THE EXPLORERS
The Story of the
Great Adventurers by Land

THE EXPLORERS

The Story of the
Great Adventurers by Land

by

H. E. L. MELLERSH

Illustrated by

PETER KESTEVEN

WHEATON
A Member of the Pergamon Group

Books in this series:

THE DISCOVERERS
THE EXPLORERS
THE DISCOVERERS OF THE UNIVERSE

Other books by H. E. L. Mellersh:

The Discoverers
Charles Darwin
FitzRoy of the *Beagle*

Archaeology, Science and Romance
Sumer and Babylon
Boy's Book of the Wonders of Man
Imperial Rome

THE EXPLORERS
Copyright © H. E. L. Mellersh 1969

First published 1969

Library of Congress Catalog Card Number: 68–19082

Printed in Great Britain by A. Wheaton & Co., Exeter
08 008740 x Hard Cover
08 008828 7 Millboard

Contents

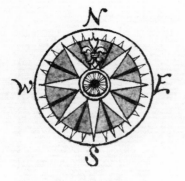

CHAPTER 1

Adventurers by land

LANDSMEN explore what seamen discover. This book, *The Explorers*, is about those adventurers by land who by their fortitude opened up for their own countrymen and for western civilization a detailed knowledge of other parts of the world.

Soldiers, sailors, courtiers, merchants, missionaries, scientists, mystics—they were a varied lot! But they were not men of common clay: they were dedicated men, passionately determined, driven on by the urge to discover. In obeying that urge they pitted themselves against the forces and deterrents of nature: the impenetrability of the jungle, the burning sands and searing winds of the desert, the unending confusions of the winding river, the

Caesar found that the Britons were intrepid charioteers in battle.

enmity of angry natives, the inhospitality of the lifeless plain, the unyielding harshness of snow and ice.

People, obviously, have moved about the face of the earth and explored it to some extent from the very earliest times: there have always been migrations in search of better lands and richer pastures, and military invasions to extend the sway of kings and emperors. But these people were all, to borrow the famous words of Thomas Gray,★ "mute inglorious" travellers; for unless you tell about your travels—and tell the story in a lasting form—you make no contribution to the knowledge of the world. The discovery of new shorelines and the descriptions of such discoveries, if only in the form of legends, do come pretty early in human history. But there are few descriptions of early penetrations inwards from the sea.

Julius Caesar perhaps deserves the name of explorer. He was a soldier and conqueror but he had the explorer's spirit. While he was subduing Egypt and dallying with Queen Cleopatra he found time to speculate on the source of the Nile, a question that was to obsess explorers nearly 2,000 years later. Without the explorer's urge Caesar might

---

★*Elegy Written in a Country Churchyard,* verse 15.

never have bothered to make his two sallies across the Channel into Britain. To exact tribute from the proud Celtic lordlings of that island would certainly enhance his prestige in Rome; militarily it might make his left flank safer. But perhaps the real urge was just plain curiosity. And plain curiosity, together with the desire and capacity to tell other people afterwards in what manner that curiosity was assuaged, is an essential ingredient in the make-up of an explorer.

Caesar wrote a famous account of his campaigns in the north, *De Bello Gallico* (About the War with the Gauls). He seems to have admired the Britons nearly as much as he admired their cousins the Gauls. He explained that in some ways they had not risen from savagery very far, that, for example, they painted themselves with woad when on the warpath; but as intrepid drivers of their chariots in battle they were marvellous.

So a Roman reported on the savages of Britain in 55 and 54 B.C., and made an economic assessment of their country. A long time afterwards the descendants of those inhabitants helped to explore the rest of the world and reported on other savages—sometimes with more perspicacity and appreciation than Julius Caesar, sometimes, unfortunately, with rather less.

The Roman empire faded and died, and the civilization the Romans had built up fell into a long decline. But at last, in the twelfth century A.D., Europe's Dark Ages were followed by a revival of learning and a rebirth of interest in the physical world—a foreshadowing of that great Renaissance of the fifteenth century, which divides medieval from modern times.

And so we come to our first great explorer, Marco Polo, a product of this twelfth-century awakening.

Julius Caesar (c. 101–44 B.C.).

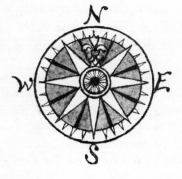

CHAPTER 2

Journey to Xanadu

"THE wonder of Marco Polo," wrote England's late poet laureate, John Masefield, "is this—that he created Asia for the European mind."

He did it at the end of the thirteenth century, by journeying to the court of Kubla Khan, ruler of the great Mongol empire, by travelling all round that empire when he got there, and by telling his story when he returned.

People have been reading *The Travels of Marco Polo* ever since. A certain Samuel Purchas read it at the end of the sixteenth century and included it in his own compilation of travellers' tales; and another Samuel, Samuel Coleridge, read Purchas a couple of centuries later, and wrote the poem *Kubla Khan*:

> *In Xanadu did Kubla Khan*
> *A stately pleasure-dome decree:*
> *Where Alph, the sacred river, ran*
> *Through caverns measureless to man*
> *Down to a sunless sea. . . .*

So do travellers' tales survive, if they have the stamp of personality and of truth.

By the early years of the thirteenth century the Mongolians, under the leadership of Ghengis Khan, had established a hold not only over Persia and all central Asia but also over the extensive territories of China. Kubla Khan, grandson of Ghengis, completed the Mongolian conquest—and found himself at the head of a vaster empire than the world had ever seen before. He elected to make the capital of China, Peking, his own capital, and accepted the ancient civilization of China as his own.

Such was the situation when in A.D. 1260 Marco Polo's father and uncle, merchants of Venice, set out from Constantinople on a trading expedition and ended up in Peking.

Marco was only six years old at that time and had, of course, been left behind in Venice. But he wrote of the expedition at second hand, in the prologue to the account of his own travels. It must have been an extraordinary adventure: one thing led to another, and the two Polo brothers followed where opportunity beckoned. If you wanted to be a successful merchant in those days you had to be adventurous; or rather, if you were naturally adventurous then a good way to indulge your bent was to be a merchant.

To visit Constantinople was purely a matter of routine for Nicolo and Maffeo Polo: Venice did more trade with Constantinople than any other port in Europe. To move on to Sudak in the Crimea was also routine, for not only was there an established trading post with the Mongols there but the Polos had a house in the town.

As business in Sudak was slack the two brothers decided to move on into Mongol territory. Carrying their merchandise in the form of jewels, a commodity of little bulk and easy to hide, they travelled 800 miles or so across the steppes to the town of Sarai on the banks of the Volga, a little north of where it flows into the Caspian sea. There they sold many of their jewels, at a profit of 100 per cent, to the emissaries of a member of the great Ghengis family. After that they were ready to go home.

But trouble and fighting broke out between two local khans and the way home was blocked. Nothing dismayed, the brothers moved on another 1,000 miles or so to Bokhara. Here they did more business and still found their way home blocked. Bokhara was very pleasant, and the danger persisted; they stayed there for three years.

In due course a person of consequence turned up on his way to the court of the great khan at Peking.

Not having ever before had an opportunity although he wished it, of seeing any natives of Italy, he was gratified in a high degree at meeting and conversing with these brothers, who had now become proficient in the Tartar language; and after associating with them for several days, and finding their manners agreeable to him, he proposed to them that they should accompany him to the presence of the great khan, who would be pleased by their appearance at his court, which had not hitherto been visited by any person of their country; adding assurances that they would be honourably received, and recompensed with many gifts.

The brothers agreed and "recommending

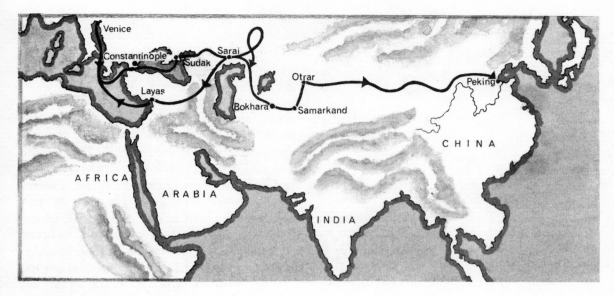

The journey of Nicolo and Maffeo Polo (1260–69).

themselves to the protection of the Almighty, they set out on their journey in the suite of the ambassador". Thus were set in train the events that led to Marco Polo's own long-extended adventure.

The Polos were not travelling in a land less civilized than their own, as was the case of most of the later explorers, but in a land where a great and ancient civilization was respected and preserved. There was a refreshing open-mindedness about these Mongol conquerors; not only did they persuade their own people to absorb the culture and the ways of China but they were also anxious to learn about other civilizations and about the Christian way of life. Kubla Khan himself evinced to the Polos a desire to know more of the western religion. "Go home to your pope," he told them, "and return with priests skilled in controversy who can prove to my people that the law of Christ is best." The two brothers were also commissioned to bring back oil from the Holy Sepulchre at Jerusalem.

The golden tablet with which Kubla armed the returning travellers was inscribed with a command that all men in his domains should help them. But even the great khan could not command the elements, and cold, snow and ice made their journey "unavoidably tedious", as Marco later put it. Nearly three whole years elapsed before the Polo brothers reached the port of Layas at the north-east tip of the Mediterranean and took ship for home.

After many delays they set out again for the east, taking with them young Marco, now a handsome lad of seventeen, and two priests—who very soon decided to turn back.

The long overland journey began through Armenia and Persia. Young Marco observed and made notes, collecting sober facts and incredible tales indiscriminately. He reported, for instance, that the ark could be seen resting on Mount Ararat—a tale that was not disproved until the difficult snow-capped mountain was scaled in 1827. But he also gave news of oil, which we call petroleum. It was not edible, he carefully explained, but it was useful as an ointment for sores on men and camels, and also for burning.

Of the rich cities of Erzerum and Tabriz, through which he passed, Marco had little to say; but to Baghdad, which had been until recently the magnificent capital of the Moslem world, he devoted a whole chapter. He described its capture by the Mongols. Hulagu, the Mongol captain, had found much wealth in Baghdad and, most spectacular of all, a tower literally stuffed with gold. Into this he also stuffed the deposed caliph of Baghdad, telling him that he ought to have put his gold to better use and fortified his capital against enemies. And, to point the moral of his tale, he left the unhappy man to starve to death amidst his useless gold. It is a gruesome story, but Marco

The journeys of Marco Polo (1271–95).

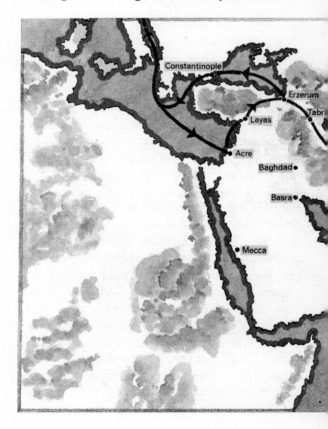

told it with some relish. His approval reflects the intense hatred that had existed between Christian and Moslem ever since the crusades, and which, as we shall see, was still in existence when Europeans began to explore North Africa nearly 600 years later.

At Saveh, Marco was shown the reputed tomb of the Magi, the three wise men who brought their gifts to the infant Jesus. He was greatly interested, and on making enquiries about the legend he was told the following story. The three wise men, in their turn, were presented with a gift by the infant Jesus. On their journey home they opened the casket they had been given and found only a stone. This stone really symbolized an exhortation to them to remain firm in their faith, firm as a rock; but they did not understand this and in disgust threw the gift down a well. The well immediately burst into flame, whereupon they took some of this fire and planted it in a temple and worshipped it. This, Marco was told, was the origin of Persian fire-worship. We moderns may prefer to think that the well from which their holy fire was first taken was an oil well.

When the travellers reached the mountain-girt city of Kerman in southern Persia two courses lay open to them. They could either strike north-east and meet the silk road, the track by which from time immemorial the silk and other wealth of the east had been brought to the Mediterranean; or they could strike due south to the base of the Persian gulf at Hormuz, where, with luck, a ship could be chartered to take them all the way round to China by sea.

The way to the silk road lay through a

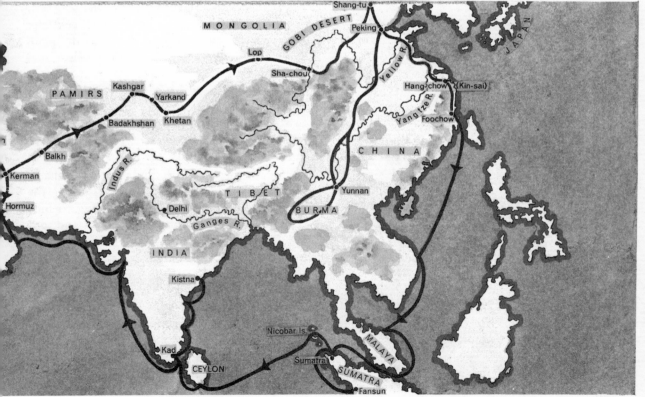

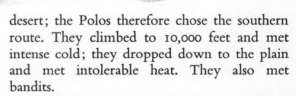

desert; the Polos therefore chose the southern route. They climbed to 10,000 feet and met intense cold; they dropped down to the plain and met intolerable heat. They also met bandits.

The Polos must have been in very great danger from these bandits. But Marco was the urbane traveller, describing in detail what he had seen and met without enlarging on his own petty personal troubles. He dwelt on the racial origin of these bandits and on a peculiarly disconcerting magic that they possessed: the ability to summon up a cloud or fog to hide their approach. He added, casually and un-emotionally, that he himself was once enveloped in an obscurity of this kind, but escaped from it to the castle of Konsalmi. Many of his com-panions, however, were taken and sold as slaves and others were put to death. The Polo party had obviously thrown in their lot with other travellers, but by luck or skill had evaded capture. As for the magic fog, we may assume that it was a natural fog of dust particles that the bandits made use of to conceal their approach. Fogs of this kind do appear in the desert to the north of the straits of Hormuz; so also does a terrible, hot searing wind which Marco also described.

When they reached Hormuz there was no boat available to take them to China. The party retraced its steps.

They now had to face the desert they had hoped to avoid. Marco, true to form, made little of the difficulties, only saying mildly that when they did find water it was bitter. Eventually they reached the town of Balach, or Balkh, and there struck the silk road.

Wild and fierce country lay in front of them. They had to cross the Pamirs, "the roof of the world", the western bastion of that huge mountain mass that is bounded in the south by the Himalayas.

The first ascent led them to a surprisingly pleasant spot, a plateau called Balashan or Badakhshan, a sort of hill station that was used by the local inhabitants as a spot for convalescing after illness. In fact, Marco said that he went there for that purpose himself and stayed in these parts for nearly a year, though this was possibly not in the course of the outward journey. He obviously enjoyed his stay on this salubrious plateau. There was falconry and there was riding, and on fine horses too—why, until recently there had been a breed directly descended from Bucephalus, the famous steed of Alexander the Great!

Now they were really on the roof of the world, ascending mountain after mountain. Believe it or not, Marco told his readers, but fires would not produce enough heat to cook their food. The fact that water boils at a lower temperature in high altitudes was one that Marco hardly expected his readers to believe; on the other hand, he recounted without apology the tale that a pillar in a certain

The young Marco Polo.

Christian church miraculously stayed up when the Moslems took away its base!

So this medieval cavalcade slowly progressed, from one lonely town to the next on the old silk road. The town of Lop was at length reached, and beyond Lop was the Gobi desert. Travellers always paused at Lop, to prepare for the ordeal in front of them.

Provisions had to be laid in for a thirty days' march and their merchandise had to be reloaded on camels, which were better than asses for desert transport. If food ran out, some of the beasts of burden could always be killed.

The real danger of the desert, according to Marco, came from the spirits that haunted the unwary traveller:

If, during the daytime, any person remain behind on the road, either when overtaken by sleep or detained by their natural occasions, until a caravan has passed a hill and is no longer in sight, they unexpectedly hear themselves called to by their names, and in a tone of voice to which they are accustomed. Supposing the call to proceed from their companions, they are led away by it from the direct road, and not knowing in what direction to advance, they are left to perish. In the night-time they are persuaded they hear the march of a large cavalcade on one side or other of the road, and concluding the noise to be that of the footsteps of their party, they direct theirs to the quarter from whence it seems to proceed; but upon the breaking of day, find they have been misled and drawn into a situation of danger. Sometimes likewise during the day these spirits assume the appearance of their travelling companions, who address them by name and endeavour to conduct them out of the proper road. It is said also that some persons, in their course across the desert, have seen what appeared to them a body of men advancing towards them, and apprehensive of being attacked and plundered have taken flight. Losing by this means the right

path, and ignorant of the direction they should take to regain it, they have perished miserably of hunger. Marvellous indeed and almost passing belief are the stories relating to these spirits of the desert, which are said at times to fill the air with the sounds of all kinds of musical instruments, and also of drums and the clash of arms; obliging the travellers to close their line of march and to proceed in more compact order. . . . Such are the excessive troubles and dangers that must unavoidably be encountered in the passage of this desert.

You may think that this was foolishness; but travellers of that time really believed it, just as sailors even two centuries later believed that they might meet boiling or coagulating seas, or topple over the edge of the world to their doom. In those days men did not think scientifically. Nor, for that matter, does science entirely absolve the Gobi desert from strange dangers and frightening phenomena. A man who has passed the whitening bones of his predecessors on the journey and is himself suffering from extremes of heat and thirst and fatigue is likely to suffer also from hallucinations. His natural fears, the tricks that mirages play upon the eyesight and the weird drumming noises made by sand blown over sand can confuse him utterly.

"When the journey of thirty days across the desert has been completed," wrote Marco, starting his next chapter in a totally unmoved manner, "you arrive at a city called Sachion." This city, now called Sha-chou, was in China proper. The religion of the people, he noted, was no longer Mohammedanism but Buddhism; and, though in his later travels he showed some appreciation of this religion in its truer form, here he described the people simply as idolaters. He mentioned a custom that later travellers also noted: the economical and optimistic burning of paper representations of cattle and goods upon a funeral pyre, rather than the valuable articles themselves.

The worst of the journey was over. The Polos struck the Yellow river, followed it northwards until it turned east in the direction of Peking, and were met there by the emissaries of the great khan. They were then conducted not to the capital but to the ruler's summer palace, in the hunting country that Kubla loved. The Polos had reached Shang-tu, the Xanadu of Coleridge's poem.

Father and uncle, Nicolo and Maffeo, had returned as they had promised. All three made their profound obeisance.

Upon his observing Marco Polo, and inquiring who he was, Nicolo made answer, "That is your servant, and my son;" upon which the grand khan replied, "He is welcome, and it pleases me much." And he caused him to be enrolled amongst his attendants of honour.

This was a surprising development. It was rather as if the Emperor Hadrian had made a Roman ambassador out of some particularly intelligent Scotsman whom he had met while inspecting his Wall, or as if Queen Victoria had made some visiting Maori chieftain a privy councillor and president of the Board of Trade. Marco Polo did, of course, come from one of the most civilized towns of medieval Europe; nevertheless, it is, on the face of it, extraordinary that this man became a highly placed civil servant, a sort of ambassador-at-large, to the great khan of the Mongol empire.

How did he manage it? No doubt essentially by being intelligent, and helpful, and likeable. He took the trouble to learn the language. He was a keen hunter and sportsman, and so was Kubla Khan. He was able to show, or to help to show, that a certain favourite of the khan's, one Ahmad, was a traitor in disguise. The khan found Marco Polo a man after his own

The great khan was a keen hunter.

heart, and to be trusted more than some of his own kinsfolk.

Marco was soon travelling widely over Asia. But first of all he observed the mode of life of the Mongols themselves and of their ruler in Shang-tu, Xanadu, the fabulous summer residence of Kubla Khan.

Shang-tu must have been something like a very grand and superior version of the present-day holiday camp, with pagoda-like pavilions instead of bungalows or caravans. The royal park was sixteen miles round, and at the entrance to it stood the khan's own palace, built of marble, "gilt and painted with figures of men and animals, beasts and birds, trees and flowers, all executed with such exquisite art that you regard them with delight and astonishment". In the centre of the park was another palace, a light and airy pavilion, constructed of lacquered bamboo and pegged down with silken cords so that it should not blow away.

And what did the khan do in Shang-tu? He was on holiday. He hunted, and in the evening he feasted. He hunted with hawks and with cheetahs, and he had a stud of 10,000 milk-white horses at his disposal. As for the feasting, what impressed Marco most was the magic that accompanied it. When the khan wanted a drink it came to him, floating through the air from the sideboard, so powerful were his magicians. Kubla was a great believer in magic and relics and the like, and in this respect was in no way more emancipated, though less fanatical, than his opposite numbers in the western world.

At the end of the summer the khan returned to Peking, making the journey in a travelling-room, specially constructed for him, on the backs of four elephants—a responsible job for the drivers! In Peking Marco experienced the more serious side of Mongol life: the business of running a vast empire. He was particularly impressed with the roads and the use made of them—the Mongols, like the Romans, knew that you cannot rule an empire without roads and the ability to move over them rapidly and efficiently. The tough little Mongols, born horse riders, were spectacularly efficient here. The quickest messengers were specially trained to endurance: at regular intervals of twenty-five miles fresh horses were waiting for them, and crack riders could cover as much as 250 miles in a day. These riders, said Marco, "gird their bodies tight, bind a cloth round their heads, and push their horses to the greatest speed".

Marco himself travelled more slowly, and also more comfortably and decorously, usually with a considerable retinue. The good roads did not always extend as far as he went, however, for he explored the furthest bounds of this huge empire as the emissary of the great khan. He penetrated eastern China as far as the coast; he went as far as Yunnan in southern China, skirting Tibet; he visited Burma and the Malay peninsula, Sumatra, Ceylon and southern India.

In eastern China Marco Polo was impressed by the ancient city of Hang-chow (or Kin-sai), the capital of the recently defeated and highly sophisticated Sung dynasty. Here he felt like a yokel come to town or a barbarian to Rome. Such magnificence! Parks and gardens; canals like those of Venice; and bridges so high that ships did not need to lower their masts. Markets where every kind of ware was sold. Houseboats on the lakes; rich people enjoying themselves; drives, excursions, picnics; the wives "very angelic, delicate things", the children so well-behaved! Hang-chow was also a great centre of culture and learning, but young medieval-European Marco was hardly equipped to appreciate that.

His journey south to the province of Yunnan took him first through a prosperous and
civilized land and then through the gorges and
along the precipices of a mountainous country
inhabited by primitive peoples. Marco was
shown a castle built long ago by a great and
splendid king who, he was told, had a little
carriage drawn not by horses but by his wives.
He saw the Yangtze river, the greatest river in
the world, and despaired of his readers ever
imagining the vast extent of shipping on its
broad waters. He heard tales of the necromancers
of Tibet, who "by their infernal art perform
the most extraordinary and delusive enchant-
ments that were ever seen or heard of". A fire
in a bamboo forest at first disconcerted him
because the giant bamboos, filled with hot air,
exploded. But then he found that travellers in
those parts made use of this and lit bonfires of
bamboos to frighten off the tigers.

On the way to Burma Marco travelled
through country inhabited by wild hill tribes
who used poisoned arrows and had a reputation
for murdering their guests. He did not say what
dangers he himself met with from these people,
but he spoke with respect of their fine horses.

In Burma itself he saw golden-roofed temples glinting in the sun and heard the sound
of bells tinkling in the breeze. He described
the great battle in which the Mongol archers
had overcome the 2,000 war elephants of the
Burmese and subdued their country. They had
been merciful conquerors and had left the
religious life and customs of the Burmese
undisturbed.

Marco travelled by sea to the Malay peninsula and Sumatra. He came down to within one
degree of the equator, and noted that the pole
star had disappeared, a most disconcerting discovery for any European. In these lands the
kings and rulers were tributary subjects of
the great khan, and their people were often

Two of Marco Polo's discoveries in Asia.

somewhat primitive. When he was delayed in
Sumatra by bad weather he had to build a fort
"to guard against mischief by the savage
natives". In these parts he discovered things that
are commonplace to us but which must have
sounded wellnigh unbelievable to his contemporaries. The natives did not make wine,
"but from a species of tree resembling the date-
bearing palm they procure an excellent bever-
age". This tree we know as the toddy palm.
Then there were nuts, the size of a man's head,
"filled with a liquor clear as water, cool, and
better flavoured and more delicate than wine".
No doubt coconut milk tastes better when it
is fresh! He came across the sago plant: "They

have also a tree from which, by a singular process, they obtain a kind of meal." This was made into "cakes and various kinds of pastries". Marco also met the rhinoceros—and people thought he was merely describing, rather inaccurately, the mythical but long-believed-in unicorn.

Up through the Nicobar islands he went and across to Ceylon (which he called Zeilan). He described, in his impersonal way, an expedition sent there by the khan to procure relics: some hair and teeth of the Buddha. We may reasonably assume that he himself led this expedition. He rose above the absurdity of his quest to appreciate something of the gentleness and beauty of the religion that Buddha had founded.

In India, however, Marco was horrified by the harsh intensity of Hindu customs: widows threw themselves onto their husbands' funeral pyres; fanatics sacrificed themselves to their gods by means of a gruesome but efficient machine, which enabled them to cut off their own heads. This was something that neither he nor his readers could begin to understand. He turned with some relief to the pearl-divers of India and to the collectors of ambergris, "which is voided from the entrails of whales" and which, as he correctly reported, served as an excellent base for perfumes.

Perhaps it was also with relief that Marco Polo, now a man in his late thirties, turned back for the court of the great khan. There he found his father and uncle anxious at last to return to Italy. Finally, in 1292, they were allowed to go; this time they made the greater part of the journey by sea.

Marco not only described the places he visited during his long stay in the east but took the trouble to find out about places that he never managed to reach. His report on Japan, for instance, had a profound influence on

Marco Polo (1254–1324).

later maritime discovery, and so on ensuing exploration.

The Mongols had been defeated in their attempts to annex Japan—one of their few failures. What cannot be had always appears the more precious, and Marco seems to have shared his master's estimation of the country he called Zipangu:

They have gold in greatest abundance, its source being inexhaustible; but, as the king does not allow of it being exported, few merchants visit the country, nor is it frequented by much shipping from other parts. To this circumstance we are to attribute the extraordinary richness of the sovereign's palace, according to what we are told by those who have access to the place. The entire roof is covered with a plating of gold, in the same manner as we cover houses, or more properly churches, with lead.

Another report of his had a profound effect on later discovery and exploration. The Mongols at one time, he said, had paid tribute to a powerful ruler who was possibly none other than Prester John, a Christian prince of the east, about whom there were already many tales and legends. The hope of finding this Prester John, of seeking his aid against the pagans, was an incentive to many adventurers.

Before saying goodbye to Marco Polo, the man who so much influenced later explorers and discoverers, take a good look at his portrait opposite. He is shown as an elderly man, benign and unworried, perhaps a little sad, self-assured but, above all, urbane and kindly.

Our next explorers, Hernando Cortes and Francisco Pizarro, had all the self-assurance of Marco Polo but little of his urbanity and kindliness.

CHAPTER 3

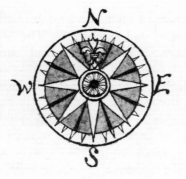

Men like gods

TWO HUNDRED years have gone by. Christopher Columbus has discovered the New World, and the doors of Europe have been opened to the wide winds of the sea—opened, too, to the hurrying wind of opportunity and the seductive wind that whispers of wealth and gold for the adventurous.

Columbus, it is well known, believed to his dying day that he had reached Asia—Marco Polo's Zipangu, perhaps, or the Indies. But it was soon apparent that something much more exciting, the whole new and unsuspected double continent of America, had been found. It was not long, naturally, before men began to explore the interior.

Two names stand out in the story of the early exploration of the new continent: Hernando Cortes and Francisco Pizarro. These

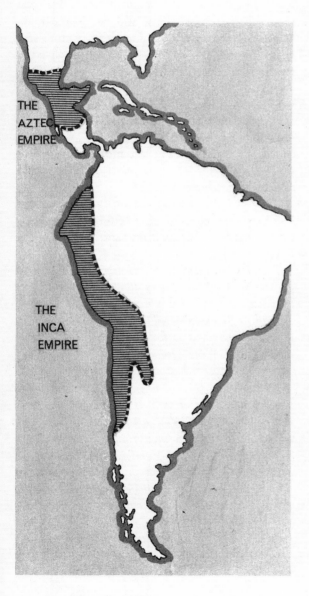

The exploration of South America began with the destruction of native civilizations.

THE
AZTEC
EMPIRE

THE
INCA
EMPIRE

men were Spaniards, for Spain was first in the field in the New World. They discovered two strange and rich civilizations, established yet primitive: the Aztec civilization of Mexico and the Inca civilization of Peru. They did more than discover them. They conquered and very largely destroyed them.

It probably never occurred to the Spaniards of the early sixteenth century to do anything but fight and conquer these people of the New World. They called themselves *conquistadores*, men of conquest. The exploration of South America by these *conquistadores* was tinged more than a little with the crimson of bloodshed.

Cortes has been credited by Keats with the first sight of the Pacific ocean:*

> *. . . like stout Cortes when with eagle eyes*
> *He stared at the Pacific—and all his men*
> *Looked at each other with a wild surmise—*
> *Silent, upon a peak in Darien.*

Keats got one thing right: Cortes was stout—stout-hearted, that is to say. But as for seeing the Pacific for the first time, Keats got the wrong man; that was another Spaniard, Balboa. The poem is, of course, about something else entirely, so perhaps the mistake does not matter very much.

Young Hernando Cortes, son of a Spanish country gentleman, started life ordinarily enough. At fourteen he went to the university of Salamanca to study law. He came away well educated no doubt, but with a decided leaning towards an adventurous life. There was only one place for Spaniards who wanted adventure and that was the New World. At nineteen Cortes found himself in Hispaniola, "Little Spain", one of the big islands off the northern coast of South America. He was

---

*In the sonnet *On First Looking into Chapman's Homer*.

25

introduced to some of the best people on the island and was given an estate and slaves to work it. It was a comfortable competence and there was not too much work. Hernando Cortes stuck it for seven years, no doubt learning in the process how to manage men. Then in 1511 he enlisted in an expedition under Diego Velazquez to subdue Cuba, the next island, which lay between Hispaniola and the mainland. The conquest was easy and Cortes remained there as chief secretary to Velazquez, who was appointed governor. Except for a quarrel with his chief—a sinister promise of things to come—there is not much news of Cortes for the next eight years. He was biding his time while others made tentative explorations of the mainland.

One of these exploratory expeditions landed on the broad peninsula of Yucatan and found there a people who were neither savage nor primitive. They came upon a town of fine stone buildings and a temple that could be rifled of gold—and it was.

At this news the Spaniards sat up and took keen notice. This was what they were looking for. There was an intense pining for gold on the part of the explorers of this century. Gold was not only the symbol of wealth but wealth itself; it was the universal medium of exchange; it was the equivalent of today's bank or treasury note, and much more beautiful.

Militarily the expedition was a failure and a tragedy. Its leader and fifty of its members died at the hands of a strong, warlike and well-armed population. But the gold ornaments remained and the memory of the dead faded. Velazquez organized another expedition. This, on landing further west, in Mexican territory, met with a totally different reception, one of ceremonious welcome. Surprised but delighted, the Spaniards exchanged a tasteful selection of glass beads for gold and jewellery worth several thousand pounds. They then penetrated a little way inland, saw a snow-capped volcano and some disturbing evidence of bloody human sacrifice, and circumspectly came home again.

A third expedition to the mainland, in 1519, was captained by Hernando Cortes. He was then thirty-two, a robust and handsome man, black-bearded, stern-eyed, with a knife-scar near his under-lip. He already possessed a reputation for stout-heartedness, but he had not easily won command of this expedition, which was intended to be a full-scale conquest and settlement. His superior, Velazquez, fearful lest all the rewards should go to Cortes, cancelled his orders at the last moment—only to find that Cortes had had wind of his decision and had already set sail.

The expedition started on a noble note. Here is the speech of encouragement that Cortes made to his men on setting sail:*

I hold out to you a glorious prize, but it is to be won by incessant toil. Great things are achieved only by great exertions, and glory was never the reward of sloth. If I have laboured hard and staked my all on this undertaking, it is for the love of that renown which is the noblest recompense of man. But if any among you covet riches more, be but true to me, as I will be true to you and to the occasion, and I will make you masters of such as our countrymen have never dreamed of! You are few in number, but strong in resolution; and, if this does not falter, doubt not but that the Almighty, who has never deserted the Spaniard in his contest with the infidel, will shield you, though encompassed by a cloud of enemies; for your cause is a just cause, and you are to fight under the banner of the Cross. Go forward then, with alacrity and confidence, and

---

*An abridged version given in *The History of the Conquest of Mexico* by William Prescott, 1843.

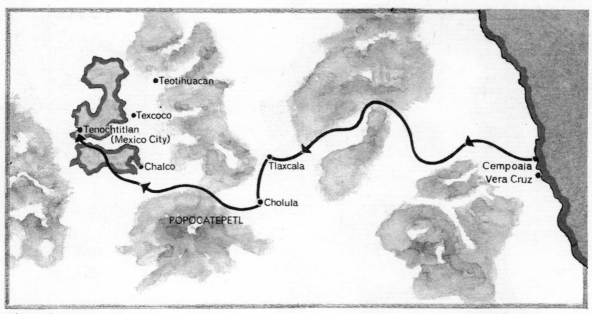

The march on Mexico City.

carry to a glorious issue the work so auspiciously begun!

This was not just a meaningless or insincere exhortation. However brutal the Spaniard was, he always genuinely desired to win over to Christianity the poor benighted natives whom he met—though the belief that a dead convert was better than a live infidel tended to make conversion a bloody process. While the Spaniards were preparing for conquest and conversion, Montezuma, the Aztec emperor of Mexico, had been waiting and watching and thinking.

The Aztecs believed, in a primitive but disconcertingly intense way, in a collection of powerful yet seldom kindly gods who lived in the heavens but controlled everything that happened upon the earth. Man's duty therefore

—indeed his self-interest—lay in doing all in his puny power to persuade the gods to exert their powers benevolently. This was Montezuma's task as high priest of the Aztecs, and he was very much disturbed by the appearance of the white men.

The chief god of the Aztecs at that time was a war god; but they had also another powerful god, on the whole more benign, called Quetzalcoatl. And Quetzalcoatl was white-skinned and bearded and had once come down to earth to visit the Aztecs, appearing from the direction of the east. Having been finally ejected by the jealous war god, he had announced that he would return in a one-reed★ year and reestablish his rule. It would be a time of great tribulation for the people.

A one-reed year was fast approaching: perhaps the white men were gods and Quetzalcoatl

---

★The Aztec calendar used a cycle of fifty-two years, and the years were named by the fifty-two different combinations of the numbers one to thirteen with four hieroglyphs: a rabbit, a reed, a flint and a house.

Hernando Cortes (1485–1547).

was among them! The second expedition of the Spaniards to the mainland had, therefore, on Montezuma's instructions, been met with great friendliness in the hope that this might propitiate the god. Now the third expedition was on its way, under the command of Cortes.

Cortes landed at the southern tip of the Mexican gulf, in the country of the Tabascans, hoping to meet the welcome given to his predecessor. But he landed a little outside the bounds of Montezuma's empire, and he had to fight. After a preliminary skirmish there followed a set battle. To win it Cortes employed strategy—and thirteen horsemen. With waving plumes and in their war paint, to the sound of trumpets and drums, the Tabascans rushed onto the Spaniards "like mad dogs". Suddenly they heard a strange sound, the sound of galloping

hooves, and they saw strange creatures, creatures with two heads, six legs and a pair of waving and avenging arms, descending upon them. The Tabascans broke and fled—surprise and fear-instilling tactics are ever the master weapons of a successful general. The chances that a force of under six hundred soldiers, fourteen cannon and sixteen horses might conquer a teeming empire did not look so impossibly small after all. The Tabascan lords made peace. Cortes acquired, amongst other things, one priceless possession: a slave woman of exceptional talent whom the Spaniards christened Doña Marina. Marina became not only a most efficient interpreter but also a staunch and courageous support to Cortes, her master.

Cortes soon left Tabasco. For four days he sailed up the coast and anchored at a spot just about 200 miles due east of Mexico City, the capital of the empire he had come to conquer. The next morning he landed. It was Good Friday. Cortes was in mourning for the death of Christ—and the Aztec prophecies had said that Quetzalcoatl would come dressed in black.

Montezuma was convinced. This white-skinned bearded man dressed in black *was* Quetzalcoatl. He fulfilled the prophecy both in his personal appearance and in the time of his arrival. It is necessary to stress that Montezuma really believed that Cortes was Quetzalcoatl, for only in the light of this belief can the strange behaviour of this serious and courageous man be understood. Cortes, for his part, never realized the depth of Montezuma's belief, never understood to the full its implications. To him the emperor of the Aztecs was simply the man who had to be dispossessed of his empire.

Cortes was ceremonially received by the emissaries of Montezuma. He, for his part, had the Christian mass celebrated in their presence and, as an additional method of impressing them, let off his cannon. He told them that he represented the great emperor, Charles V; that he had arrived with friendly intent and to trade; and that he would like to come to see their capital and king.

Hurrying back, the emissaries reported to Montezuma. When he heard that Cortes-Quetzalcoatl wanted to come to his capital he almost fainted. He greatly feared the fulfilment of the part of the prophecy that promised great tribulation. But he was also a faithful servant of the war god and he regarded the approach of the returning god with dismay. Of course, if it came to a show-down Quetzalcoatl would have to be obeyed. But first of all he sent back the emissaries with instructions to use all their arts to dissuade the visitor from coming to Mexico City.

The Emperor Montezuma.

29

The emissaries returned with certain professional wizards and enchanters who exercised their own particular brand of dissuasion, though there is no sign that Cortes even noticed what they were trying to do. What he did notice, and his men too, were the rich gifts that were meant as a compensatory peace offering, but which only served to whet the Spanish appetite for conquest.

Nevertheless, three months were to elapse before Cortes marched upon Mexico City. He knew a good deal more by then. He knew that in some way the Aztecs worshipped him as a god, and that, since their gods were devils, this advantage would have to be exploited very circumspectly. He knew that the Aztecs conducted their fighting so that they might take prisoners, and that the fate of all such prisoners was to be sacrificed to their terrifying war god, who fed on still-beating human hearts torn from living bodies. He knew that Mexico City stood in the middle of a lake, and that it could only be approached (or, for that matter, retired from) by causeways that could easily be disrupted.

While he made his preparations some of Velazquez's friends and partisans among his officers put it to him that the expedition ought to return. They had won a goodly show of gold from Montezuma's presents, they said, and to think of conquering the country with their present small force was madness. Cortes had two reasons for not going back. One was that he was determined to do nothing of the sort and believed implicitly in his own chances of success. The other was that if he returned he might find himself clapped into jail for disobedience. Characteristically, Cortes acted with both decision and guile and turned the awkward position to his own advantage.

First he threatened the Velazquez clique with the stocks or the gallows for intended mutiny,

and at the same time he talked the rest of his soldiers into a state of enthusiasm. Then he bethought himself of his legal training at the university and devised a brilliant scheme for ridding himself of Velazquez's overriding authority. If he were to turn his military camp into a municipality, he could, as head of that municipality, claim to be directly subordinate to the Spanish crown. No sooner thought of than done! Though they can hardly have noticed the difference, his followers changed overnight from soldiers in a camp to citizens of a municipality, and Cortes began writing humble and circumspect reports of his doings to his new master the Emperor Charles V, king of Spain.

Cortes's new municipality was on the edge of the country of the Totanecs, a people who were subject to Montezuma and most unwillingly so. Cortes cultivated their friendship. Then when tax-collectors came from the emperor demanding twenty girls and boys for sacrifice as a penalty for helping the white man, Cortes boldly had the tax-collectors seized and imprisoned. He assured the half-overjoyed, half-frightened Totanecs that he would protect them against any reprisals, and offered them a military alliance, which they accepted. He then released the tax-collectors and sent them home with a message informing their master who it was who had released them. Then, with the best of both worlds well gained, Cortes made his final preparations for his advance into the interior.

On 15 August 1519, 300 *conquistadores* set out. Before them fluttered a banner of black velvet emblazoned with gold, on which was written in Latin, below a red cross set amidst flames of blue and white, "Friends, let us follow the Cross; and under this sign, if we have faith, we shall conquer." A small rabble of Totanecs accompanied them, acting as guides and porters.

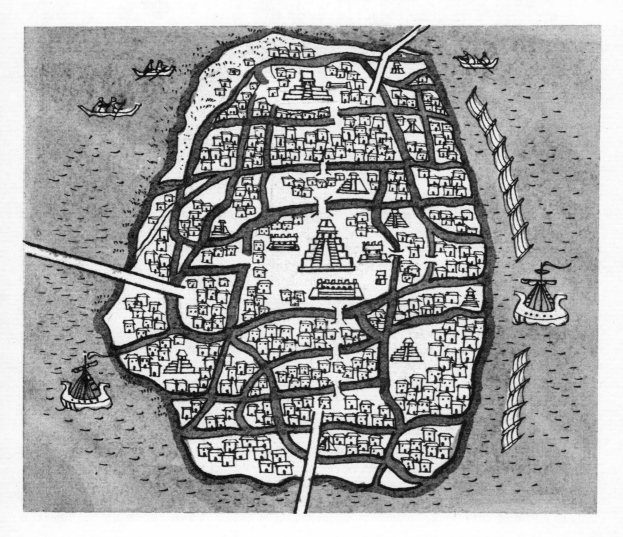

Mexico City—the "Venice of the Aztecs".

The massacre at Cholula.
(Based on an Aztec drawing.)

Along the 250-mile path to Mexico City lay Aztec strongholds, stony ravines and rushing rivers, a desert of volcanic ash, and passes at 10,000 feet between mountain peaks higher than any in Europe.

Up in the mountains the cold was intense. Some of the Indians died, but not the Spaniards. Through the treeless waste they marched and then, exhausted and half-starving, they descended into a small Aztec city, where they received only a lukewarm welcome. A little boasting improved the position. While his men extolled their leader's greatness Cortes also was busy, impressing the lords of the place. Were these creatures, his horses, dangerous? He said that they were, very. And his dogs? "As bad as jaguars."

Another seventy miles or so and the Spaniards came to a greater city, where something more than boasting was needed. They had come to the country of the Tlaxcalans, who were not subjects of Montezuma's empire but were continually attacked and used as a sort of reservoir of living victims for the Aztec war god. The Tlaxcalans, naturally, were the deadly enemies of the Aztecs.

The Tlaxcalans at first showed no desire whatever to become the allies of Cortes. They engaged the Spaniards in a long-drawn battle—and when one brave Tlaxcalan with a double-handed sword managed to decapitate a horse and prove that the creatures were mortal and not magic, things looked particularly black for the Spaniards. They held on, until eventually a Tlaxcalan chief was killed and the tide of battle turned. The Indians sued for peace, and the very fact that a desperate battle had been fought increased their respect for the Spaniards and their desire to make amends. Cortes had won an ally.

At this point the Spaniards were three-quarters of the way to Mexico City. Fresh emissaries from Montezuma arrived. "He sent word," Cortes informed his new master, the king of Spain, "that I should say how much I wanted to give Your Highness as an annual tribute of gold, silver, precious stones, slaves, cotton, mantles and whatever else might be acceptable. He would give all that was asked, if only I would not visit him in his city." As well give a hound a sniff of the quarry and then expect him to turn back! Cortes resumed his march, but now with 6,000 Tlaxcalans behind him.

Cholula was the next place reached, an Aztec town wholly subject to Montezuma. The presence of the Tlaxcalans made the Cholulans suspicious. Cortes sensed that he was going to be attacked, and, true to character, struck first. 3,000 perished, so Cortes reported, and the Tlaxcalans, feeling they had done enough, returned home loaded with loot.

Montezuma, now accepting the inevitable, stopped trying to bribe Cortes to turn round and invited him to come to Mexico City, where he would be well received. Cortes proceeded with a lighter heart when he knew that he could enter the fortress as a guest and not have to force his way in.

In the relief afforded by this invitation Cortes encouraged his men in a feat of genuine and peaceful exploration: the scaling of Popocatepetl, a volcano of almost 18,000 feet. The fact that his native guides pronounced it impossible no doubt made the conquest all the more desirable. They almost reached the top, but sulphurous fumes and flying cinders were more successful than Aztecs in holding back the *conquistadores*.

Cortes resumed his march. Soon they were at the edge of the mountain plateau and saw spread out before them the beautiful valley of Mexico, or Tenochtitlan as the natives called it. In the distance shone a great lake; and, in the words of Prescott, in the middle of the lake there lay "like some Indian empress with her coronal of pearls, the fair city of Mexico, with her white towers and pyramidical temples, reposing as it were on the bosom of the waters—the far-famed 'Venice of the Aztecs' ".

The Spaniards were about to enter it unopposed, indeed invited. Was Montezuma in his senses?

It is impossible for us to understand Montezuma's agonies of indecision and involved superstition-ridden calculations. He was a haunted man in a terrible predicament. The returned Quetzalcoatl must be obeyed. Yet must he, Montezuma, really give up his throne to him? And if so, how could it be done without catastrophe? Could he carry his people with him in effecting the change? And how could the great war god be appeased?

Events moved relentlessly to a climax. The two leaders first of all lived side by side as friends; the Spaniards were guests and were treated royally, and were much impressed with the royal dignity, wealth and luxury of Montezuma and his court. Moreover, Cortes found himself in the position of ruler-designate of the empire, for Montezuma told him that he was willing to resign in his favour.

Yet nothing happened. Montezuma took no step to make Cortes ruler in fact. The Spanish leader found himself living in a sort of vacuum and he was not the person to be satisfied with that. Three events stimulated him to action. The first—following a tour of the war god's temple, which horrified him—was Montezuma's refusal to become a Christian. The second was the accidental discovery of a room in the palace given over entirely to the storage of

Cortes and his men threw down the idols.

treasure. The third was the news that the Spaniards' base had been attacked; and this, he could only assume, was with Montezuma's connivance.

Cortes acted with his usual ruthless decision. Montezuma was imprisoned.

The imprisonment was, of course, most gently done, and Montezuma was allowed all his old pomp and ceremony. It was real enough, however. In his new and tragic situation Montezuma comported himself with the utmost dignity; and all the Spaniards who came in contact with him felt pity and admiration.

Yet it was obviously a dangerous step to have taken. Would the Aztec people, the Aztec lords, acquiesce? They did not. A revolt started, but was immediately quashed. Cortes had the ringleaders executed.

Montezuma, in no one knows what agony of soul, asked to be allowed to go to worship his god. Permission was given, so long as he made no human sacrifices. He disobeyed. Cortes then insisted that all human sacrificing should stop and that the Cross and a statue of the Virgin should replace the idols. Montezuma temporized. Cortes and some of his men went to the temple and, in the presence of the priests, threw down the idols.

That was a courageous and humanitarian thing to do. But it was also extremely rash; it made the final tragedy inevitable. Montezuma was told unequivocally by the lords of his council that the war god demanded the destruction of the Spaniards and that they, the said lords, would see to it that the people obeyed their god. Montezuma passed on the stark news, and suggested that Cortes had better go. Cortes temporized in his turn, realizing the seriousness of the position: his ships had been destroyed—let some more be built then. Montezuma agreed.

35

At this point, an avenging army sent by Velazquez arrived in the country. Leaving Alvarado, one of his lieutenants, behind with eighty men, Cortes sallied forth from Mexico City to defeat the forces of Velazquez. In spite of having the smaller army he succeeded. But when he returned he found that Alvarado, less circumspect than himself, had precipitated an Aztec revolt and had only with great difficulty been able to contain it.

The return of Cortes merely aggravated the situation. Fighting broke out again and the Spaniards found themselves besieged in the royal palace where they had their quarters. Montezuma, at his own request, went out onto the walls and pleaded with his people to cease the fighting and accept their Quetzalcoatl-Cortes lord. He was greeted with a shower of sling stones, one of which felled him to the ground, mortally wounding him. With genuine sorrow the Spaniards watched him die.

After that their position rapidly became untenable. Back across the causeways, fighting a fierce rearguard action, they went. Mexico City was once more free from Spaniards.

The end? Of course not, for Cortes was Cortes. Now he made real and effective use of his Tlaxcalan allies. He retreated among them, worked up their fighting enthusiasm and returned with an invincible host. In August 1521 the wonderful city on the lake was destroyed. Cortes was master of the Aztec empire.

Two years later, royally appointed as Captain General of Mexico, or New Spain, sure of his conquest and relaxed again, Cortes ordered another attack on the only thing that remained unconquered, the volcano Popocatepetl. He had the satisfaction of conquering that also.

Later he led an expedition into Honduras, and then another across to the coast of southern California. Then he settled down as marquess of the valley of Oaxaca, where he had rich estates and many slaves, and set about rebuilding Mexico City in Spanish style.

36

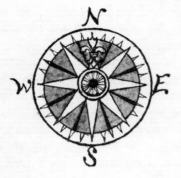

CHAPTER 4

El Dorado

THE obsession with gold that so moved the *conquistadores* created its own myth: the story of El Dorado, which means the golden or the gilded one. Mostly it was a golden city that men talked about; sometimes it was a golden man, an emperor who year by year was ceremonially sprayed with gold dust and descended into the waters of a sacred lake where, year by year, he left behind him a shining patch of gold.

The efforts of Francisco Pizarro were in a general sort of way a search for El Dorado. His discoveries lent particular strength to the fable and inspired other adventurers who, in their turn, helped to explore the central and western regions of the great double continent of America.

37

Pizarro was himself inspired by the example of Cortes. He won for Spain the great empire of the Incas of Peru; it was larger and, in some ways, more highly civilized than the Aztec empire of Mexico. Nevertheless Pizarro had not the stature of Cortes. He was a Cortes without humanity. He was the gold-seeker personified; he had courage without compassion, efficiency without understanding, lust without light.*

His chief victim was Atahualpa, emperor of the Incas of Peru, whom he captured by a trick, whom he condemned to be burnt at the stake, whose mode of death he commuted by his boundless mercy to strangulation as a reward for his conversion to the Christian faith, and for whom on the next day he put on the clothes of mourning.

The scene of this story is set in the cold, bleak and rarified altitude of the Andes, the southern section of the long lopsided mountain backbone of the Americas. Francisco Pizarro first approached the Andes in 1524, three years after Cortes had conquered Mexico. He was then forty-eight years old and had already seen much adventure. He had begun life as a swineherd, then he had become a soldier and fought for Spain in Italy. Then the New World called him. He was one of the band who with Balboa in 1513 first set eyes on the Pacific from a mountain peak in Darien. He joined an expedition to Panama, the purpose of which was to trade with and to subjugate the natives. He

stayed on there and fed his hungry soul with rumours of wealth that existed for the taking beyond the mountains to the south.

Then came news of the success of Cortes in Mexico; this was something to be emulated. With borrowed money, and with the permission of the governor of Panama, Pizarro and a certain Diego de Almagro, destined to be his lifelong companion and his enemy, set out on an expedition. They went by sea to seek out this rich civilization that was said to exist beyond the mountains. It was a miserably unsuccessful expedition. They discovered little but mangrove swamps, alligators, and natives who ran away from them. They found no El Dorado. Pizarro was not discouraged, however. He determined to go farther next time.

Two years later he set off again. After appalling hardships, he at length crossed the equator and sailed on down a pleasanter coast to find the rich and stone-built town of Tumbez. This was the outpost of the civilization he was seeking. Here Pizarro heard for the first time of the Inca, the great ruler of this civilization. He also heard rumours of internal strife such as had existed amongst the enemies of Cortes—and he no doubt allowed himself an anticipatory smile. He then took away some of the wealth of Tumbez and returned to his governor at Panama with optimistic proposals for a more ambitious expedition.

The governor turned down Pizarro's proposals; so Pizarro did what others had done

---

*Southey wrote a poem in the form of an epitaph on the conqueror of Peru. It begins:

> *Pizarro here was born: a greater name*
> *The lists of glory boast not. Toil and pain,*
> *Famine and hostile elements, and hosts*
> *Embattled, failed to check him in his course.*

It ends, addressing the reader, thus:

> *However wretched be thy lot assigned,*
> *Thank thou, with deepest gratitude, the God*
> *Who made thee, that thou art not such as he.*

Francisco Pizarro (c. 1478–1541).

before him: he travelled back to Spain to put
his case before his king. On arrival he was
clapped in gaol for an old and, so far as he was
concerned, forgotten debt.

Then his luck changed. Cortes himself was
in Spain, and Cortes befriended him and pro-
cured for him his interview with the king.

Pizarro showed King Charles the jewels from
Tumbez; he showed him the beautiful wool of
the alpaca llama; he enlarged on the magnificent
opportunity here for the king to convert yet
another pagan empire to Christianity. He
got permission to conquer Peru. Orders were
given, and a certain amount of financial help, to
fit out an expedition for that purpose. One
morning in January 1530, Pizarro set sail from
Spain with three undermanned ships. A year
later, having refitted in Panama, he landed on
the Peruvian coast near the town of Tumbez.

Pizarro's march into the interior and his bold
dealing with South America's greatest native
emperor was similar in some respects to the
effort of Cortes in Central America. The Inca
people were hardly less superstitious in their
religion than the Aztecs, though by no means so
bloodthirsty; the mountains were as difficult as
those in Mexico, and the risk of encirclement
and defeat as dangerous. But Pizarro, unlike
Cortes, had little help from any native convic-
tion that he was a returned god; there are,
admittedly, indications of some such belief but
it had little significance. On the other hand, he
was greatly helped by the internal situation in
the Inca empire and by the past sins of his
adversary. Whereas Montezuma had made
enemies of some of his neighbours, Atahualpa
had made enemies among his own people, for
he had usurped the throne and had plunged his

39

country into civil war. The rumours of disunity that Pizarro had heard at Tumbez were true. Pizarro was determined to make full use of his advantage.

Atahualpa had just been successful in defeating and imprisoning his half-brother; he stood, therefore, at the head of a well-found and lately victorious army. Pizarro and his little band of adventurers had to go cautiously. But these *conquistadores* with their guns, their unbelievable horses, their incredible self-assurance, seem to have inspired an incapacitating fear in the hearts of those who faced them.

Yet not all the 170-odd men were as self-assured as their leader about the march across the mountains. Even in the comparatively easy and friendly country of the foothills there were some with faint hearts. Pizarro, becoming aware of this, talked to his men. There was still a chance to turn back, he said, for those who wished to do so—he could do with a bigger garrison at his base. No doubt with these conciliatory words his eye roamed fiercely. Nine men in all elected to return. Thus purged, the rest went on.

Pizarro was relieved to receive a report from one of his lieutenants whom he had sent on to deliver a message of friendliness to the Inca. Atahualpa, he said, was with his army outside the sizable town of Caxamalca on the further side of the mountains; he would be glad to receive the white man in audience. "God ever fights for his own," Pizarro told his men. "And no doubt he will humble the pride of the heathen, and bring him to knowledge of the true faith, the great end and object of the conquest." With that noble sentiment—in which, to be fair to him, he may well have believed—Pizarro mounted his horse, unfurled his banners and assaulted the colossal heights of the Andes.

For a while the little army traversed a

BOUNDARY OF
INCA KINGDOM 1532
ROUTES OF SPANISH CONQUERORS ━━

The conquistadores *in Peru.*

magnificent road, which, though it impressed them with the might and efficiency of the enemy, did at least also make matters easy.* But then the road turned in the wrong direction. Could they not continue to follow it, some asked—it might lead to gold. But they did not ask for long. Nor did they dare to blench, except inwardly, at some strung-up figures that Atahualpa's army had left behind. Across great rocky fissures, along the edges of dizzy precipices, they proceeded. The land was sterile, the cold intense, and their only companions were the soaring condors waiting with gruesome optimism for their flesh.

Another messenger who had been sent on ahead by Pizarro reported that Atahualpa was sending an emissary to meet them. This Indian nobleman came, with gifts, smooth words and the roaming eye of a spy. The interview ended with an effort by each side to impress the other —by what William Prescott calls a game of brag.** Pizarro realized that the Inca recognized him for what he was, an implacable foe. He proceeded warily.

At length, on descending the mountains, the Spaniards saw in the distance the stone buildings of Caxamalca glistening white in the sunshine. Across the valley another sight faced them: a host of tents, as thick as snowflakes, the camp of Atahualpa's army. "The spectacle," wrote one of the *conquistadores*, "caused something like confusion and even fear in the stoutest bosom. But it was too late to turn back or betray the least sign of weakness." On entering Caxamalca, they came upon a situation almost equally unnerving: the streets echoed to the Spaniards' footsteps; the town was completely empty. It had been deserted.

Pizarro occupied the town in businesslike fashion, installing his men in the best building, the emperor's local palace. He then sent a deputation to Atahualpa.

There ensued another bout of fencing with words and efforts to impress. Pizarro's chief messenger, a cavalier named de Soto who was renowned for his horsemanship, gave an exhibition of his prowess. He made his horse gallop full tilt at Atahualpa and come to a halt so close to the emperor that he was flecked with its foam. But Atahualpa did not flutter an eyelid. Some of his soldiers did show fear, however, and the emperor was able to display his splendid discipline by having them promptly executed for cowardice. He sent back the Spaniards with a message that he would call upon Pizarro on the morrow, with his chieftains. The deputation returned, somewhat depressed; their depression increased when the falling night revealed to them the myriad camp fires of their enemy.

Pizarro held a conference of leaders. He had already determined what to do: when in a tight corner he would act like Cortes and be bold. He would, he explained, hide his men around the central square of this town they were occupying. Atahualpa and his chieftains would enter and would be met with ceremony. Pizarro's chaplain would offer the Inca the chance to embrace the Christian faith and swear fealty to the Christian monarch, the Emperor Charles V. If he were to refuse—and no one could have expected him to do anything else—then the hidden Spaniards would attack at a given sign. It was a desperate plan. But it was agreed to.

The next morning, having seen that his troops

*The Inca rulers had learnt the same lesson as the Mongol khans, that you cannot administer a large empire without good roads. They, too, used a system of express messengers.

**Prescott followed up his book *The History of the Conquest of Mexico* by another, and some think a better, *The History of the Conquest of Peru*.

were well fed and well prepared, Pizarro had
mass celebrated with great solemnity. All
joined with enthusiasm in singing the chant,
"Rise, O Lord, and judge thine own cause."
"One might," wrote William Prescott, allowing himself a bitter criticism for once, "have
supposed them a company of martyrs, about to
lay down their lives in defence of their faith,
instead of a licentious band of adventurers,
meditating one of the most atrocious acts of
perfidy in the record of history!"

From their places of hiding the Spaniards
watched the brilliant procession approach. The
emperor was borne aloft in a litter on the
shoulders of his nobles, and these were so
richly apparelled that, as one of the watchers
said, "they blazed like the sun".

But then, on nearing the city, the procession
halted and the emperor sent a message that he
would encamp outside for the night. This did
not suit Pizarro's plan at all. He had worked up
the fighting spirit of his men and he could not
afford to let it evaporate. He therefore begged
the emperor to change his plans and to come
and sup with him.

The emperor accepted. Why did he? Was he
mad, mesmerized, or just plain curious and
foolhardy? He did at least bring down his
soldiers to ring the city. Perhaps it never
occurred to him—to him, great Atahualpa,
lord and conqueror of an empire—that he
could really be in danger from this handful of
adventurers.

All went according to plan, with a sickening
inevitability. Atahualpa entered a silent city. His
retinue was enormous but unarmed. They
arranged themselves around the square. "Where
are the strangers?" asked Atahualpa of his
nobles. Then Pizarro appeared with his chaplain
and interpreter. A disquisition on the Christian
faith was followed by the somewhat imperti-
nent request that the Inca should acknowledge

Atahualpa's entry into Caxamalca.

himself a subject of Charles V. Atahualpa understood enough. His eyes flashed and he made an indignant refusal, pointing proudly to his own god the sun—which, Prescott points out, was then sinking. The priest handed a Bible to the emperor. Atahualpa turned its pages, then let it fall to the ground. The scandalized priest turned to Pizarro. "I absolve you!" he cried. Pizarro waved his white scarf, giving the signal for attack.

"Saint Iago and at them!" the *conquistadores* cried. From one quarter came the swordsmen and musketeers, from another the horsemen, from another the shot from Pizarro's artillery, a pitifully small force but deadly enough in this confined space. It was a massacre. The royal litter swayed and finally fell. One noble after another shielded the emperor with his unarmed body, but all their courage was of no avail. The emperor was taken prisoner, and with the news of his capture, all resistance, not only inside the town but outside as well, came to an end. The Inca empire was no more.

Atahualpa had nine months to live, Pizarro nine years. They were neither happy months nor peaceful years. Atahualpa, in his prison chamber, boasted that if he were freed he would have the room filled with gold—"Yes, right up to here," and he jumped up with arm outstretched. Pizarro took him at his word, and Atahualpa had the room filled with treasure up to the red line that was drawn to mark his offer. The value of Atahualpa's treasure was perhaps £2,000,000. But he gained nothing by it, for the Spaniards did not keep their side of the bargain. Atahualpa had become a liability, a possible focus of rebellion, and so they tried him for conspiracy, rebellion and sacrifice to false gods. The outcome has already been told: he was condemned to be burnt at the stake but, on becoming a Christian, was promoted to death by strangulation.

There was one rebellion by the Incas. It was unsuccessful. But before long the conquerors were fighting amongst themselves over the rewards apportioned to them by the king of Spain.

Almagro, Pizarro's original companion-in-arms, was made ruler of a large province to the south. But how does one define exact boundaries in an unknown land? Quarrelling was inevitable. Almagro, after making a heroic trek across the mountains and deserts of his new land, a trek on which most of his men died, struck northward to Cuzco, the capital city of the Incas. This did not belong to him and he had to be ousted. Pizarro, who was in Lima, his own new capital in the north, sent two of his brothers to do the job. They did it thoroughly; they not only defeated Almagro but had him tried and executed for treason. But Almagro left behind him a son and a fanatical following; and these, coming north, entered Pizarro's palace and murdered him. So in 1541 the old soldier and explorer—and, more recently, the builder and administrator of fine cities—came to a miserable end.

It was initially something less romantic than gold that set Pizarro's youngest brother Gonzalo on the quest for El Dorado. Pizarro, only a little while before his assassination, sent him off to the very north of the Inca empire with instructions to explore eastwards. There, it was believed, he would find in abundance the trees that yielded one of the world's most valuable spices, cinnamon.

Gonzalo set off with enthusiasm. Spices were the next best thing to gold, and he had little difficulty in recruiting followers. He started with 350 Spaniards, 150 of them on horseback, and 4,000 Indians. Behind them went a large trotting larder—a drove of swine.

Starting from the Inca town of Quito, almost exactly on the equator, they first of all crossed the Andes. The cold and the icy winds struck into them and many Indians died. They experienced an earthquake. Then at last they plunged down into a totally different world of winding rivers, swamps and jungles.

It was not an easy world for a marching army—and that is an understatement. Moreover, they had arrived in the rainy season. Their swords rusty, their provisions spoiled, their clothes almost rotting off them, Gonzalo and his men did indeed find the cinnamon trees. And that, officially, was the end of their quest. But they were lured on by a tale they heard: the natives of that region said that at ten days' distance there was a rich and populous land, abounding in gold. Rashly they went forward.

For a while the way was easier. But then again the tropical forest closed in. They hacked their way through. The swine had gone by now, but they had some hunting dogs with them and there were still some horses. These they ate one by one.

45

At length they came to a broad expanse of water and, beyond it, to an awe-inspiring cataract which thundered down to a narrow rushing river far below. They followed the river. Finding no populous and rich country on their side of the river, they resolved to build a bridge and explore the other side. The forest there seemed much the same, but natives insisted that there was a fruitful country only a few days down the river, so the Spaniards continued.

Their river now became navigable. If they could build a bridge, they could build a boat. There was plenty of timber. They spent two months building a boat large enough to carry all their baggage and half the Spaniards. For some days they progressed side by side, the fit marching and the sick in the boat. They ate toads and snakes and such food as they could

win from passing natives. The promises that constantly lured them on now changed a little in form: the rich and prosperous people lived where the river they were following joined a greater river, the Amazon. Gonzalo decided to send on the boat to this point, so that it might collect provisions and return. The cavalier Francisco de Orellana was given command. With fifty companions he set off.

For weeks Gonzalo and his men waited for him, but in vain. At last they determined to push forward on foot to the confluence of the two rivers. It took them two months to reach the place, a journey that the boat had accomplished in three days. They found a country that was indeed more populous but very little more inviting. They also had news of the boat and its captain from one of the party who had been marooned for insubordination. Disbody: difficulties encountered in the right spirit were half defeated already.

They took a more northerly course home, and it was in truth less beset with difficulties, though, as Prescott points out, they were in less good shape to meet any difficulties, great or small. Eventually they returned to Quito, the Indians of their party reduced in number by one-half, and the Spaniards by three-quarters. "Such was the end of the expedition to the Amazon," wrote William Prescott; "an expedition which, for its dangers and hardships, the length of their duration, and the constancy with which they were endured, stands perhaps unmatched in the annals of American discovery."

And Orellana and his men? Whether they had deserted or simply bowed to the inevitable may be argued but hardly decided. They went on down the great river.

They met rocks and rapids and escaped, as it seemed to them, by a series of miracles. They met hostile natives who sometimes chased them for miles in their canoes, and sometimes with bows and arrows prevented them from landing and obtaining food. Some of these warriors had long hair. The Spaniards thought they were women and, remembering the ancient Greek fable of a race of Amazons, they called the river (which had perhaps some similar-sounding native name) the Amazon. At last they had better luck and a native chief fed them with partridge and parrot; Orellana in return supplied spiritual food and delivered a dissertation on the law of God and the might of the Spanish emperor—after which he took possession of the land in the emperor's name. Finally they reached the coast and sailed on to Trinidad, and from there Orellana took ship across the Atlantic to tell his tale to his king.

One of the party wrote down the story. And he did what was no doubt expected of him and

covered half-naked and wandering in the forest, he had a tale to tell that struck dismay into the hearts of Gonzalo and his companions. Orellana, having found neither supplies nor friendly people, and knowing it to be impossible to return by the river against the current, had deserted them all and sailed on down the Amazon.

Greatly discouraged, the unhappy band struggled onwards for a few more days. Then Gonzalo decided that they must turn round and make their way back to Quito. The prospect must have appalled his men, but Gonzalo appealed to their reason, and even more to their pride as Castilian Spaniards. He promised them a different way home, which he believed would be better. For the rest—and here he touched on the very essence of exploration in any age—the spirit he said, would maintain the stressed in his tale the intimations of great wealth they had met with, wealth that only by the greatest ill luck they had missed. They had seen messengers from a distant kingdom, richly dressed and adorned with costly ornaments. They had heard about the golden city of Manoa where the Incas, fleeing from the wrath of Pizarro, had taken their wealth.

So the El Dorado legend was strengthened, and many adventurers set off to search for the wonderful city of Manoa. One of Cortes's lieutenants, Diego de Ordaz, the conqueror of Popocatepetl, explored along the Negro, a great tributary of the Amazon. Other adventurers explored the Orinoco. Jiminez de Quesada started out from the new Spanish colony in what is now Colombia and followed the river Magdalena up into the foothills of the Andes. He made there a discovery and a conquest comparable to those of Cortes and Pizarro, though far less well known.

To begin with, Quesada's expedition followed the usual pattern. A body of sword-bearing *conquistadores* attacked the jungle in fantastically inappropriate clothes, with the wrong food, without proper equipment for exploration—with nothing but their own amazing spirit to drive them on. Then out of their dark nightmare they came into a wide and smiling valley and to uplands rich with plantations of maize. They had reached, entirely by chance, the home of the Chibcha Indians, a people in some ways as civilized as the Incas, skilled in rich and delicate metal-work and in the building of stone temples to their sun god.

But, like the Incas, the Chibchas were divided amongst themselves, and the Chibcha empire—twice the size of France—fell into Quesada's hand like a ripe plum. Quesada hurried home to his king to ask that he might be made governor of these lands he had discovered and begin the task of converting the

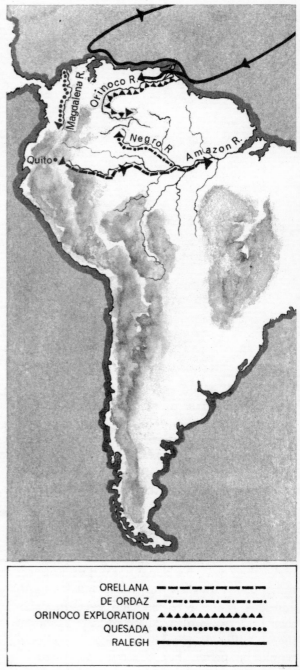

ORELLANA	– – – – – – – –
DE ORDAZ	–·–·–·–·–·–·
ORINOCO EXPLORATION	▲▲▲▲▲▲▲▲▲▲▲
QUESADA	●●●●●●●●●●●●
RALEGH	——————————

The quest for Eldorado.

Chibcha people, for whom he had a real liking. But through court intrigue and favouritism the post he so confidently asked for went to the son of the governor of Colombia.

Quesada's discovery merely whetted men's appetite for gold, as the failure of others merely strengthened their obstinate resolve. The myth of El Dorado would not die. Nearly sixty years later an Englishman, none other than Queen Elizabeth's famous courtier, Sir Walter Ralegh, was continuing the quest.

If Quesada was a soldier-saint, Ralegh was a soldier-dreamer. From the days of his earliest contacts with English sailors the idea of the New World had fascinated him. But he saw it differently from many of his contemporaries. There across the ocean lay not only wealth, not merely heathen to be converted, but lands to be lived in—new and splendid lands that could become possessions of his beloved queen, fresh jewels in her crown.

His colonizing efforts in North America we shall touch upon in the next chapter. But even in South America when, like the Spaniards, he was searching for El Dorado, there was this difference. He always treated the natives with consideration because he saw his compatriots later living with them; and he always had an eye for natural beauty and natural fertility as well as for gold.

But gold, always gold: do not let us imagine that the magnificent Walter Ralegh was altogether different from his contemporaries. His expedition made its way up one of the tributaries of the Orinoco, in the territory of present-day Venezuela, where it borders on Guyana. Ralegh had the good sense to go by boat and not on foot, and to glean all information possible before he started—including some from a Spanish gentleman whose garrison he defeated but who seemed to bear him no ill will. But, for the rest, the expedition had much

Sir Walter Ralegh (c. 1552–1618).

49

the same tale to tell as many of those before it: steaming heat and hardship; the occasional meeting with a minor chieftain richer and more friendly than the rest; rumours of riches that never materialized; the captain of an exhausted crew urging his men on further and just a little further. It is a tale, however, that has great interest because the sensitive Ralegh himself told it.* Here is his description, often quoted, of a happier part of the journey:

On both sides of this river we passed the most beautiful country that ever mine eyes beheld; and whereas all that we had seen before was nothing but woods, prickles, bushes, and thorns, here we beheld plains of twenty miles in length, the grass short and green, in divers parts groves of trees by themselves, as if they had been by all the arts and labour of the world so made of purpose; and still as we rowed, the deer came down feeding by the water's side, as if they had been used to a keeper's call.

There Ralegh met a local chief whose wife had hair that reached down to the ground. It was arranged "in pretty knots". "I have seen a lady in England so like her," he wrote, "as but for difference in colour I would have sworn might have been the same."

One of the natives gave him an armadillo, "which seemeth to be all barred over with small plates, somewhat like a rhinoceros, with a white horn growing in his underparts, as big as a great hunting horn, which they use to wind instead of a trumpet."

One day he made an important discovery. He had gone in search of four natives who had retreated from their canoes into the forest. "As I was creeping through the bushes," he wrote, "I saw an Indian basket hidden, which was the refiner's basket, for I found in it his quicksilver, saltpetre, and divers things for the trial of metals, and also the dust of such ore as he had refined."

It must have been the memory of this last discovery that encouraged the disgraced Ralegh, many years later when he was a prisoner in the Tower, to make a final desperate bid for rehabilitation and freedom. In 1617 he was freed and allowed to set off once more for the Orinoco in search of gold. The expedition was unrelieved tragedy. His son was killed; his greatest friend committed suicide; nothing was achieved. When Ralegh returned he was sent to the block at the command of the suspicious and vindictive James I, on an ancient and trumped-up charge of treason, aggravated now by the sin of failure.

By the time of Ralegh's death the conquest and—not to put too fine a point upon it—the destruction of the great Aztec and Inca civilizations was complete.

Not all the Spaniards were destroyers; there were many devoted men who tried to make the lot of the defeated native less hard and to preserve their history, their art and their traditions. Yet few explorations have been more cataclysmic, more quick and overwhelming in their effect, than those made in Central and South America, where the explorers were the *conquistadores*, the conquerors.

---

*It is often printed in the last volume of Ralegh's *History of the World*, a book still to be found in the libraries of most of England's great houses, and indeed in almost any library that dates back to the 17th century. The 1829 edition of this work is on the reference shelves of many public libraries.

CHAPTER 5

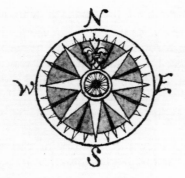

Lakes, rivers and Red Indians

NORTH AMERICA was not particularly inviting to the adventurers of the sixteenth century. When mariners landed—and it was not, generally speaking, an easy coast on which to land—they found no natives with gold ornaments to whet their appetites for plunder, but only primitive savages. The land sometimes had the appearance of great fertility, but that was not what adventurers were after. They wanted easy money.

Sir Walter Ralegh was an exception. He dreamt of establishing a prosperous English colony on this fertile land.

As Queen Elizabeth would not let her favourite courtier go himself on such a colonizing expedition, he had to be content to organize it. First he sent out two captains to make a reconnaissance. They landed near the mouth of the Roanake river and found the native Indians friendly and accommodating. One chief's wife acted like any kindly farmer's wife, washing the Englishmen's clothes for them and seeing that their feet were bathed. She did more. When the Englishmen were startled by the entry of armed warriors she made the warriors break their bows and arrows across their knees. The king of the country, who was called Wingina, was equally friendly.

The captains brought back to Ralegh a glowing report. Making a pun on the name of Wingina and a pretty compliment to his queen at the same time, he announced that the new colony should be called Virginia. He then had a new coat of arms made for himself whereto the title "Lord and Governor of Virginia" was added, and forthwith organized a colonizing expedition of seven ships. The year was 1585. Again Ralegh was not allowed to go and he proposed Sir Philip Sydney as the leader. Finally Sir Richard Grenville went.

Everything started beautifully. This is how Ralph Lane, the man left in charge of the colony, wrote home:

In the meanwhile you shall understand that since Sir Richard Grenville's departure from us, as also before, we have discovered the main* to be the goodliest soil under the cope of heaven, so abounding with sweet trees that bring such sundry rich and most pleasant gums, grapes of such greatness, yet wild, as France, Spain, nor Italy hath no greater. . . . To conclude, if Virginia had but horses and kine in some reasonable proportion, I dare assure myself, being inhabited with English, no realm in Christendom were comparable to it.

Yet when a supply ship from the homeland arrived a year later there was not a single

Ralegh sent out two captains to make a reconnaissance.

*i.e. the mainland.

Englishman to be found. Francis Drake with a fleet of tall ships had passed by, and the colonists, already at loggerheads with the Indians, had clamoured to be taken home.

It was a bad beginning. But before Ralegh's death the first of the English colonies, or plantations, had been successfully established on the eastern seaboard. This colony, Jamestown, was in Ralegh's Virginia and owed much to the earlier efforts of that vital dreamer.

Captain John Smith was the first head of the colony of Jamestown and he carried out considerable exploration from this base. He also wrote at length about his doings. It is obvious that some of his stories were highly coloured, but on the whole they gave a circumstantial and accurate description of the ways of the Indians. One of his most famous stories is about the beautiful Indian princess, Pocahontas, and how she saved the life of Captain Smith.

One day, when exploring a long way from home, Smith became separated from his men and was attacked by Indians. He put up a brave fight and, with some presence of mind but not much kindness, forced his native guide to act as a body-shield. In spite of this he was, to use his own words, "shot in his thigh a little and had many arrows that stuck in his clothes but no great hurt, till at last they took him prisoner".

They took him to their chief for judgement. Here at the Indian settlement they fed him so well that he believed he was being fattened for a cannibal feast. Then they held a dancing ceremony round him "singing and yelling in such hellish notes and screeches; being strangely painted, everyone his quiver of arrows and at his back a club". Then he was made to sit in front of a great fire, "and presently came skipping in a great grim fellow, all painted over with coal mingled with oil, and many snakes' and weasels' skins stuffed with moss and all their tails tied together, so as they met on the crown of his head in a tassel". The witch doctor's dance over, Captain Smith was brought into the presence of the chief. This great man, having washed his hands and dried them on a bunch of feathers, feasted while his victim waited, and then at length caused Smith to be seized and his head laid on two great stones. Above Smith towered large men with clubs.

It was then that the chief's dearest daughter, Pocahontas, came to the rescue. She took poor Smith's head in her arms and laid her own protectively upon it. The sentence of death was duly commuted and Smith was exchanged for a couple of the white men's cannon and a corn-grinder. As for Pocahontas, she herself was later taken prisoner and came to the white men's settlement, where she married one of them, a Mr John Rolfe. In 1616 she sailed to England with him, and there, after one brief year of our unkind climate, she died.

The rivers that John Smith explored had all led him up against the Alleghany mountain barrier. He believed optimistically that the Pacific coast was not very far beyond this.

Some years later Abraham Wood, a gentleman of Virginia who prospered in the fur trade while his compatriots in England were battling through the Cromwellian civil war, sent out an expedition across the Appalachian mountains (of which the Alleghanies are a part) in the hope of finding an arm of the Pacific ocean reaching inwards from California. What the expedition found in the end was a tributary of the Mississippi. But they also found, carved on two trees, the half-obliterated and quite unknown names of white men, fur-trappers perhaps, who had been there before them—a reminder to us of all the unknown and unsung explorers who followed adventure in their everyday business.

The French explorers of North America

Pocahontas in England.

were also convinced of the nearness of the Pacific coast. When Jacques Cartier was sailing up the St Lawrence river in 1536 the Indians of that region told him of great seas that were not so very far away. No European knew of the great lakes at this time, and so the great seas were taken to mean the Pacific ocean on the other side of the continent.

Jacques Cartier went back and told his king, who was duly impressed. But nothing practical was done until sixty years had gone by, as France was engaged in bitter internal religious wars and in wars against Spain. Not until the seventeenth century could she afford to cast her eyes overseas. Meantime, however, she retained an interest in North America, and French fishermen made an excellent living from the swarming seas around the St Lawrence estuary and traded with the coastal Indians for furs.

In 1603 Samuel de Champlain, geographer to the French court, set off for the St Lawrence estuary. His king wanted him to increase the possessions and the prestige of France; the rich men at court wanted him to increase their wealth through an expansion of the fur trade; and Champlain himself wanted to increase his own considerable prestige as a traveller through further exploration and discovery. Rather naturally the third desire took precedence.

The French, in marked contrast to the Spanish, usually succeeded in getting on well with the native Indians. Champlain excelled at this. He was not too proud to learn from them, and they respected and admired him for it. For over ten years, off and on, he explored the country around Quebec, where he founded a white man's settlement. His culminating triumph was his penetration into lake Huron, which he called the sweetwater sea. He entered it not by way of the other lakes, Ontario and Erie, but by striking due west up the river Ottawa. He and his five companions went by canoe. It was a difficult journey despite Champlain's cheerful description of it.

One difficulty was that North American rivers had a habit of breaking into rapids and tumbling over waterfalls. Interminably Champlain and his companions had to hump their canoes instead of riding on them, and of course they had to hump all their belongings too. 250 years later a Canadian farmer's boy ploughed up a little cache of silver cups and copper kettles and an astrolabe (an early type of sextant), which had almost certainly been left behind with reluctance by this exploring party.

Champlain found this region a "frightful and abandoned" one, but admitted that God had given it slight compensation in an abundance of wild raspberries and blueberries, fruit that the natives dried "just as we do plums in France for Lent". Less of a compensation were the fleas they found in every village!

But this determined explorer and humane gentleman got on very well with the natives, who, he said, went out on special fishing and hunting expeditions so that they might "entertain us as daintily as they could". And as for the fish, Champlain asserted that he had seen trout as much as four and a half feet long—a fisherman's tale that can never now be verified. One tribe of Indians he particularly admired. He

called them the High Hairs, "because they had them elevated and arranged very high and better combed than our courtiers, and there is no comparison, in spite of the irons and methods which these [the courtiers] have at their disposal. This seems to give them a fine appearance. . . . I gave a hatchet to their chief who was as happy and pleased with it as if I had made him some rich gift."

In one native village, to his surprise and delight, he came across one of the Catholic missionary priests whom he had persuaded to come out with him from France. Here was advance not by the cross and the sword but very much by the cross alone. Sometimes these devoted missionaries met hatred and misunderstanding and torture and death. But sometimes, by showing the best in themselves, they evoked the best from the Indians. If this was not always conversion it was at least a deep, though possibly somewhat puzzled, admiration.

In their intrepid wanderings the French missionaries were, of course, also exploring. The most famous of them was Jacques Marquette, the Jesuit father who, some sixty years after Samuel de Champlain's work in North America, was roped into an official exploration.

By then France was efficiently administering the colony of New France from its capital, Quebec. The great-lake system had been pretty well explored, but still there was no sign of the Pacific coast.

The French, anxious to extend their dominion, were hopeful that some of the many rivers rising to the south of the great lakes might flow westwards and guide men to the Pacific coast. We know now, of course, that these were the Mississippi and its tributaries, and that they flow south into the Atlantic.

An official by the name of Louis Joliet was instructed to find out if there was a way to the

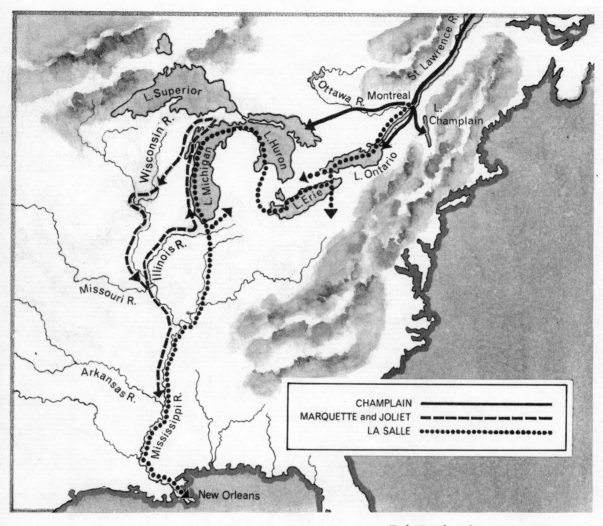

Early French explorations in North America.

Pacific by these rivers; and he, very sensibly, sought out Father Marquette who was in charge of a mission at the western extremity of lake Superior and knew a great deal about the tribes in that area. In 1673 the two of them set out hopefully down the river Wisconsin, recommending themselves to God and imploring his help. It was an anxious journey. Father Marquette was perfectly well aware of the ferocity of many Indian tribes, and every tribe they met warned them of the ferocity of their neighbours.

But if ever an explorer benefited from a reputation for kindness, and a convincing air of serene gentleness, Father Marquette was that man. It enabled him not only to proceed but to observe.

One day, having paddled for a long way without meeting a soul, the exploring party espied human footprints on the bank. Marquette and Joliet determined to follow them. They came at length to an Indian village. Should they go on, the pair of them, unarmed and unprotected? They prayed, and went on. As they approached the village they could hear the Indians talking. Here is Marquette's account of their reception:

We then deemed it time to announce ourselves, as we did by a cry, which we raised with all our strength, and then halted without advancing any further. At this cry the Indians rushed out of their cabins, and having probably recognized us as French, especially seeing a black gown, or at least having no reason to distrust us, seeing we were but two and had made known our coming, they deputed four old men to come and speak with us. Two carried tobacco pipes well-adorned and trimmed with many kinds of feathers. They marched slowly, lifting their pipes towards the sun, as if offering them to him to smoke, but yet without uttering a single word.

Like all Jesuit missionaries, Father Marquette had taken much trouble to learn the local languages. He asked these four solemn men who they were, and they understood and replied

that they were Illinois Indians. They offered their pipes to the two white men, to be smoked in the accepted gesture of peace. They then escorted them, with much ceremony, into their village.

At the door of the cabin in which we were to be received, was an old man awaiting us in a very remarkable posture; which is their usual ceremony in receiving strangers. This man was standing perfectly naked, with his hands stretched out and raised towards the sun, as if he wished to screen himself from its rays, which nevertheless passed through his fingers to his face. When we came near him, he paid us this compliment: "How beautiful is the sun O Frenchmen, when thou comest to visit us! All our town awaits thee, and thou shalt enter all our cabins in peace." He then took us into his, where there was a crowd of people who devoured us with their eyes, but kept a profound silence. We heard, however, these words occasionally addressed to us: "Well done, brothers, to visit us!"

That was the Red Indian at his best, dignified and impressive, responding peacefully to peaceful overtures. There followed a meeting with the Illinois chief and then a feast, for which, like all travellers in strange countries in any century, they needed strong stomachs. They were pressed to take the daintiest morsels, which were held before their mouths: the fare was dog, accompanied by boiled meal seasoned with grease!

They passed from the Wisconsin to the Mississippi and found that this river persisted in heading for the south, contrary to all their hopes and expectations. Marquette and Joliet followed it downstream for well over 1,000 miles, then, when they were past the latitude of 35°, they came to the conclusion that the Mississippi must without doubt flow into the gulf of Mexico and not into the Pacific ocean. They turned back.

Two things on their journey had particularly impressed them. In one place they had seen huge native rock paintings of strange beasts (this was long before the discovery of Stone Age cave paintings in France) and they were quite unable to believe that these were done by local and savage artists, since "good painters in France would find it hard to do so well". The other sight that impressed them was the rushing turmoil of water—dangerous as well as impressive—where the great river's greatest tributary, the Missouri, came in from the west.

Father Marquette believed that if he were to follow the Missouri to its source, then he would come very near to the Pacific ocean. He was perfectly right.

The brave and gentle priest was never able to test his theory, for two years later he died. Nor did anyone else explore the Missouri to its source for over a hundred years.

Robert de la Salle followed Father Marquette down the Mississippi, and travelled extensively over the whole area from the Mexican gulf to the great lakes, staking out claims for France. He was a difficult and emotional man, not always successful, but always willing to learn from the Indians. And the particular lesson he learnt was that it was possible to abandon dependence on the river and the canoe and to cover great distances on foot. One journey that la Salle performed was an epic of its kind. With a few companions, none of whom did the whole journey, he traversed the 1,000 miles from Fort St Louis on the Illinois river to Fort Frontenac on lake Ontario, through snow, ice, slush, mud and tangled woods, carrying nothing with him but a gun, a bag of corn and a supply of leather for the repair of his moccasins.

For the next hundred years the European powers were almost constantly at war. One bone of contention, and a pretty big one, was the control of North America. The French were in the north, the Spanish in the south, the English (with a sprinkling of Dutch and Swedes) were in those multiplying plantations along the eastern coast, the first of which had been established under Captain John Smith. In the middle lay the vast fertile plains of America watered by the great rivers; and beyond them, still unknown and unexplored, the Rocky mountains barred the way to the Pacific coast.

Robert de la Salle (1643–87).

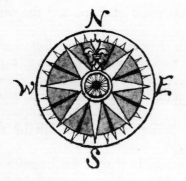

CHAPTER 6

"Go West, young man"

IT IS bad luck for a writer to be remembered by only one sentence he has written. Such a fate befell the early-nineteenth-century American journalist Horace Greely, who is remembered solely for this single piece of advice: "Go West, young man, and grow up with the country!" It was popular advice. This was just what his compatriots wanted to do. Throughout the nineteenth century they went West in their thousands.

The first man to pioneer a way to the West was Alexander Mackenzie, an employee of one of the great fur-trading concerns, the North West Company. Like all genuine explorers, he was more interested in discovering new territory than in anything so mundane as the search for more and better furs. Nevertheless he was a loyal servant to the North West Company, and, in turn, the company gave him enlightened support.

Alexander Mackenzie wanted to be the first man to travel across the northern continent all the way from the eastern coast to the western. He had been brought up in the northernmost of Scotland's Western Isles and this in itself was a tough enough school of experience. It was followed by several years at the company's lonely outpost on lake Athabaska, where the handsome and commanding young man learned everything the older trappers could teach him.

On 3 June 1789 he set out on his journey. He was then about thirty-four years old. He took with him a crew of five trappers in one large birch-bark canoe and in another five Indians, including a guide and interpreter accompanied by his two wives. On the first day they covered thirty-six miles and on the second eighty-one; Mackenzie drove his teams hard. Soon they reached the Great Slave lake. Even at this time of the year they found it covered with broken ice, and were in perpetual danger of having their canoes crushed. Plagued also by mosquitoes, they searched for an exit towards the west.

There they found a river, which now bears Mackenzie's name. With a strong current and a following wind to help them they raised their sails and happily launched themselves upon it. For 300 miles it carried them westwards. Then disconcertingly, the Rocky mountains loomed up ahead of them, and the river turned north.

Still hopeful, they continued to follow the river. Natives told them that there was a sea to the west, but they warned the white men that it would probably take a lifetime to reach it, and that they would meet horrible monsters and men with wings who could kill by the piercing glance of their eyes.

When Mackenzie next took his bearings he realized that he had come so far north that he was only one degree from the Arctic circle and that almost certainly the river he was following would end not in the Pacific but in the Arctic ocean. He pressed on nevertheless; and duly reached the northern ocean. Then he turned back and, in a race against approaching winter, arrived home in just three months from the start of his journey. He had covered 3,000

Alexander Mackenzie (c. 1755–1820).

miles, but he had not reached the Pacific coast.

Mackenzie was as determined as his compatriot Robert the Bruce. Feeling that he was not as well equipped as he ought to be, either materially or mentally, he went back to Britain to prepare himself for his next attempt. There he collected instruments and fortified himself with a better knowledge of geography and surveying, and then returned to his fur trader's post for another attempt.

This time he followed the Peace river, which reaches westwards from lake Athabasca. The trouble was that this river flows into the lake and not out of it, and this meant a struggle against the current from the start.

Mackenzie and his men struggled for 500 miles, and then once more the Rocky mountains faced them.

They soon came up against new difficulties. It is the habit of most Rocky mountain rivers not only to flow swiftly but to gouge out deep canyons for themselves. The Peace river had now become a mountain river, and it was running true to form. There was nothing for Mackenzie and his men to do but brave the rocks and the rapids and press on. Every now and then they got out and mended their canoes.

They came at last to a fork in the river, one branch of the stream going due north, the

Mackenzie's search for a route to the west coast.

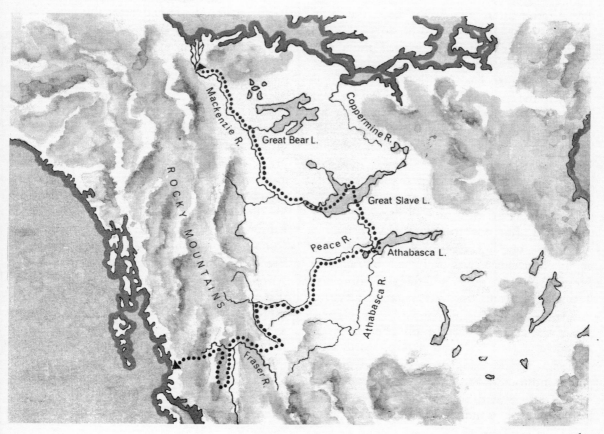

other due south. Which were they to take? The northerly stream looked the more inviting, but the local Indians advised the southerly. Mackenzie took their advice, and it proved to be sound.

But the river petered out. Portage across to another river was the answer, he was told. He obeyed. He went on, and found the river Fraser.

He continued down the Fraser but at last became convinced that he was travelling the wrong way, though he had been warned that the approach to the sea by this river was very long and very difficult. His men were frightened and discouraged. He knew, like Cortes on his way to Mexico City, or Ralegh on the interminable Orinoco, that it was his authority and his determination alone that kept the little band together. What should he do?

He assembled his men, praised them and warned them, and then announced that he intended to turn back up the Fraser and find a way to the coast on foot. To his relief his men took it well—they had sufficient faith in his leadership and in themselves. They turned back, stowed their canoes and set off. After a fifteen days' march they reached the Pacific coast. For the first time Europeans had crossed the wide north American continent from coast to coast.

It was a great achievement, deservedly acclaimed. But one trip does not discover a continent; one line across a map does not fill it in. Mackenzie was followed by another servant of the same fur-trading company, David Thompson, who was an expert surveyor and map-maker.

By 1814 David Thompson had made an excellent map of a large part of north-west America, and he had not found it an easy or unadventurous job. Sometimes he travelled over the snow with sledges and dog teams, but neither the dogs nor the men driving them were very expert. His men often refused to let certain landmarks out of their sight because they were not used to the compass and did not trust it. This is the explorer's everlasting dilemma: if he goes unaccompanied, he goes without help; if he goes with a party he has to put up with delays and inefficiency.

David Thompson's business in north-west America had been primarily to persuade a particular tribe of Indians to enter into trade with his company. These were the Mandan Indians who lived round the head-waters of the Missouri river, and it is to the Missouri river that we must now turn.

You will remember that Father Marquette had believed that the exploration of the Missouri might provide an approach to the Pacific coast. The initiative for this exploration came at length not from one of the European powers, nor from an ambitious trading company, but from the government of the newly independent American colonies. After the war of Independence the Americans had time to look around. They were particularly interested in distant California; they heard reports of its wealth in furs and that other nations approaching California from the Pacific ocean were gleaning that wealth. Thomas Jefferson, third president of the United States, was impressed by the reports of a certain John Ledyard, a flamboyant but knowledgeable gentleman of Connecticut whom we shall meet again in a later chapter; he determined, therefore, upon action. He proposed to the American congress that an exploring party, provided with military support, should penetrate up the Missouri river to its source and then cross the highlands and follow the best water communication that offered itself from there to the Pacific.

The accounts of the expedition give an impression of cheerfulness, efficiency and confidence—virtues that were needed before it reached its goal. First, it took all its equipment on specially built river barges down the Ohio from Pittsburgh and then up the Missouri to the land of the friendly Mandan Indians. There the expedition wintered. The next spring it set off in smaller boats and canoes to penetrate up the Missouri into the Rockies.

The party consisted of the two leaders, Captain Meriwether Lewis and Lieutenant William Clark, with twenty-six soldiers, one French-Canadian hunter, one Negro servant and an Indian guide, together with the guide's wife, who carried a baby, strapped Indian-fashion on her back. This papoose, Pomp, or Pompey, was to become a great favourite, and was soon learning to entertain the company round the camp fire by clinging to his mother's fingers and dancing to the tune of a violin.

The first part of the journey was fairly easy, almost monotonous at times, so that to go out hunting for game was a privilege, in spite of the danger from snakes and grizzly bears. Buffaloes, too, could be dangerous; on one occasion a buffalo suddenly charged straight through the camp, but luckily no harm was done. The explorers passed through the Bad Lands, where bare sandstone hills had been weathered into fantastic shapes. They met dust storms. They waded through icy water. They discovered the great falls of the Missouri. Then they came to the mountain divide, and here they tried to get horses from the local Indians for the middle stage of their journey.

The task was not easy. The Indian tribes were having a war amongst themselves, as they so often did, and were suspicious of everyone, whites included. Captain Lewis needed all his determination and tact—and he had a good deal of both.

The trouble was that the Indians kept on retreating before the hopeful and well-intentioned military party and made themselves

65

T.E.—E

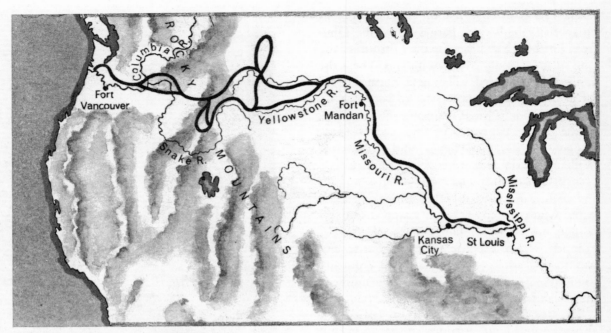

The exploration of Lewis and Clark (1805–06).

as scarce as rabbits at the sound of a gun. At length, by chance, two squaws were isolated. This is how Captain Lewis, in an entry in his diary dated Tuesday 13 August 1805, describes what happened next:

They appeared much alarmed but saw that we were too near for them to escape by flight. They therefore seated themselves on the ground, holding their heads as if reconciled to die, which they expected no doubt would be their fate; I took the elderly woman by the hand and raised her up, repeated the word tab-ba-bone, *and stripped up my shirt sleeve to show her my skin; to prove to her the truth of the assertion that I was a white man, for my face and hands, which had been constantly exposed to the sun, were quite as dark as their own. They appeared instantly reconciled, and the men coming up, I gave each woman some beads, a few moccasin awls, some pewter looking-glasses and a little paint. . . .*

After they had become composed I informed them by signs that I wished them to conduct us to their camp, that we were anxious to become acquainted with the chiefs and warriors of their nation. They readily obeyed and we set out, still pursuing the road down the river. We had marched about two miles when we met a party of about sixty warriors, mounted on excellent horses, who came in nearly full speed. When they arrived I advanced towards them with the flag, having my gun with the party about fifty paces behind me. The chief and two others who were a little in advance of the main body spoke to the women, and they informed them who we were and exultingly showed the presents which had been given them. These men then advanced and embraced me very affectionately in their way, which is by putting their left arm over your right shoulder clasping your back, while they apply their left cheek to yours and frequently vociferate the word ah-hi-e, ah-hi-e, *that is, I am much pleased, I am rejoiced. Both parties now advanced and we were all caressed and besmeared with their grease-paint till I was heartily tired of the national hug.*

So, in due course and after a lot of pipe-smoking ceremony and delicate negotiation, they got their horses. Pomp's mother was a great help, as she came from this particular tribe, and so also, to a lesser extent, was the Negro with his black skin and crinkly hair, who seems to have been shown to the Indians as an intriguing freak of nature.

Now came the greatest trials of the whole journey. Only a few days before, a trooper had walked with one foot on each side of a dramatically diminished stream and thanked God that he "had lived to bestride the Missouri". But here, in this barren land of peaks and canyons, all jokes were forgotten. The explorers lost their way in snowstorms. The only food they had was dried soup, bear-oil, and horse-flesh when they could bring themselves to shoot one of their spare mounts. Scurvy, the scourge not only of the sailor but also of everybody else who has to live on an unnatural diet without fresh foods, began to show itself.

At last they found their way across and travelled down the mountain slopes towards the sea. Their troubles were not over; they merely became unheroic. The change to a moist soft air deprived them of all their remaining energy; the change to a diet of salmon upset their digestion; and the west-coast Indians were thieves and flea-ridden.

On 8 December, just nine months after setting out from their Mandan winter base, the men were again building themselves new winter quarters. Their clothes were rotting and much of their food had gone bad. At Christmas they had only pulverized fish for dinner. But Captain Meriwether Lewis, giving the lie to circumstances by his name and vigorous leadership, wrote cheerfully, "We were awaken-ed at daylight by a discharge of firearms, which was followed by a song from the men, as a compliment to us on the return of Christmas."

So by men like these the pioneer work of exploring the northern continent was largely done. And after them other white men went out and settled, spreading thinly across the vast plains and onto the rich west coast of North America.

This movement to the West began in the 1840s. It is a story familiar to us in the "Westerns" of film and television. It was a sort of mass exploration—it was *family* pioneering. These young men who followed Mr Greely's advice to go West—yes, and old men too and mothers with babies—really blazed the trail.

Because the treks were family affairs, covered wagons were used. It might have been quicker to travel on horseback, but there would have been no shelter, no travelling-home for the family. Many a woman who knew that a baby was on the way set out for the West, and many a baby was born in a covered wagon. The long line of mules or lumbering oxen had its disadvantages, but these were more than outweighed.

A typical trek is described by George R. Stewart in *The Californian Trail*, a book that has the appropriate sub-title, "An Epic of Many Heroes."

This trek has come to be known as the trek of Stevenson's party. It set off in 1844 under the command of Elisha Stevenson, an ex-blacksmith and a born leader of men. The party eventually reached a beautiful lake in that part of the Rocky mountain range known as the Sierra Nevada (Sierra means saw-edged) and they could find no way forward but up a bare granite slope, rising steeply more than 1,000 feet.

They decided to leave half the wagons

behind. The rest they unloaded, and then carried everything, the young children included, to the top. Next they hitched a double yoke of oxen to each empty wagon and, one by one, began the ascent.

Halfway up there was a vertical ledge ten feet high. Here they nearly gave up. But they discovered a narrow rift in it where one ox at a time could get through. One by one the bulky and protesting beasts were unhitched and pushed through the gap. Then on the sloping scree they were reharnessed with longer chains, and with every man helping at the wheels the wagons were heaved up the ledge.

Three men volunteered to stay with the wagons they had elected to leave behind, on the promise that they would be rescued next spring. But with the winter came snow so deep that hunting, by which they had hoped to keep alive, became impossible. Two of the men followed after the main party, and did in fact reach safety. The third decided to stick it out. By learning to trap foxes he managed to stay alive, and in the spring, true to promise, he was rescued.

Here, to end with, is a description of a situation familiar to readers and viewers of "Westerns". It is taken from Mr Stewart's book.

The wagons are drawn into a circle. Around them gallop the Indians on their ponies, shooting arrows. From the shelter of the wagons, the men fire their rifles. Children cower in the wagon boxes, and women crouch with them or load rifles for the men. Indian after Indian tumbles from his pony . . .

But do not get excited!
"I have told no such story in this book," the author continues. He goes on to explain that, though it may have happened like this, he can find no evidence of Indians ever being so foolhardy. What they did do was to attack the wagon train when it was strung out on the march, and, if the tight circle was then formed, they laid grim siege to it, preventing any white man from escaping to find water. This method was more efficient, and more terrifying in prospect to men and women setting off on the long trail to the West.

CHAPTER 7

Timbuctoo is not just a name

WHEN words and phrases become household jokes we may be sure that originally they must have hit the nation's consciousness good and hard. "Oh, go to Timbuctoo!" people used to say, when they had occasion to wish you to a place that was remote and inaccessible. Bishop Wilberforce, wishing to be amusing, wrote:

> *If I were a cassowary*
> > *On the plains of Timbuctoo*
> *I would eat a missionary,*
> > *Coat and bands and hymn-book too.*

Such a funny word, Timbuctoo!* Where is it? In Africa?

---

*Timbuktu is the modern spelling, but the nineteenth-century form is used in this chapter on nineteenth-century African exploration.

Until the end of the eighteenth century Africa remained virtually unexplored by the western world. From the time of Christopher Columbus onwards ships had continually sailed along the African coasts; but these coasts were singularly unwelcoming, with few natural harbours. Moreover Africa was regarded by European mariners and discoverers as merely being on the way to somewhere else—the fabulously attractive east.

One of the first British explorers of Africa was the Scotsman James Bruce. He was a wealthy and cultured man, a student of Arabic and particularly interested in the antiquities of the North African coast. In 1768 he visited Egypt and from there set off to discover the source of the Nile, that mysterious river that flows for 1,000 miles without a tributary and regularly once a year floods its banks and spreads tons of fertilizing mud and silt over the farmlands of Egypt.

He took ship from Egypt to Abyssinia, or Ethiopia, and spent some time in that country. His account of his travels was later published and did a great deal to stimulate a new interest in the continent of Africa.

The civilization of Abyssinia claimed to be Christian, but it was in many ways remarkably savage, cruel, bloodthirsty and primitive. One of the first things Bruce saw when he reached the Abyssinian capital was a group of men tethering a cow, cutting a slice off its haunches, sewing up the wound, and eating the raw flesh. This was one of the many things that the powdered, periwigged and sophisticated gentlemen of England would not believe when they read Bruce's book. One of them, breaking into verse, remarked neatly:

Nor have I been where men (what loss alas!)
Kill half a cow and turn the rest to grass.

There were other things about the Abyssinians that Bruce found highly unpleasant, not least their methods of waging perpetual and pointless war. He was glad to get away at last on the mission that had brought him to these parts, the finding of the source of the Nile.

He set out with a large retinue of porters and a colossal quadrant for determining latitude, and at length reached lake Tana. Beyond the

An Abyssinian chieftain.

71

lake, in charming, flowering country, he came upon a swamp, and within the swamp was a little hillock. "Throwing my shoes off," Bruce wrote later, "I ran down the hill, towards the little island of green sods." Reaching it, he stood in rapture. "It is easier to guess than to describe the situation of my mind at the moment, standing in that spot which had baffled the genius, industry and inquiry of both ancients and moderns, for the course of near 3,000 years." He believed that he had found the source of the Nile.

But had he? Unfortunately, no. At Khartoum the Nile splits into two, the Blue Nile and the White Nile. The White Nile is by far the greater river, and Bruce had followed the Blue. He had also travelled too far, for lake Tana itself is strictly the true source of the Blue Nile. And, moreover, another European, a Jesuit priest, had been there before him in the preceding century.

We need hardly feel sorry for Mr Bruce, however; he was too self-sufficient a man to need anyone's pity. We must certainly not discount the significance of his own great contribution to exploration.

On his way back from the source of the Blue Nile, Bruce took a different, and more difficult, route. Like Marco Polo, he crossed a desert. It was the Nubian desert, the eastern offshoot of the great Sahara. Here he heard none of the mysterious whispering or booming voices of the Gobi desert, but he encountered the *simoom*, the wind that seemed to carry a furnace within itself and which all who knew the desert rightly feared. He later described how Idris, his guide, saw the signs of the approaching wind from afar off and took action:

Idris cried with a loud voice, "Fall upon your faces, for here is the simoom." I saw from the S.E. a haze come, in colour like the purple part of the rainbow, but not so compressed or thick. It did not occupy twenty yards in breadth and was about twelve feet high from the ground. It was a kind of blush upon the air and it moved very rapidly, for I scarce could turn to fall upon the ground with my head to the northward, when I felt the heat of its current plainly upon my face. We all lay on the ground as if dead, till Idris told us it was blown over. The meteor or purple haze which I saw was indeed passed, but the light air that still blew was of heat to threaten suffocation.

Bruce had traversed one of the hottest parts of the world. In his account of his travels he explained carefully to the uninitiated the effects of varying degrees of heat:

I call it hot when a man sweats at rest, and excessively on moderate exertion. I call it very hot, when a man, with thin or little clothing, sweats much, though at rest. I call it excessively hot, when

a man in his shirt, at rest, sweats excessively, when all motion is painful, and the knees feel feeble as if after a fever. I call it extremely hot, when the strength fails, a disposition to faint comes on, a straitness is found round the temples, as if a small cord was drawn round the head, the voice impaired, the skin dry, and the head seems more than ordinary large and light. This, I apprehend, denotes death at hand.

Bruce led his readers to understand that he had experienced personally all these degrees of heat. Not everyone believed him.

One of the few people who took James Bruce really seriously was Sir Joseph Banks. He had gone with Cook on the *Endeavour* in 1768 as a naturalist and had later become president of England's, if not the world's, foremost scientific institution, the Royal Society.

He was also a member of a much more lowly institution called the Saturday Club, the purpose of which was nothing more than to dine once a week in London, at the St Albans Tavern off Pall Mall. Such clubs were fashionable at this time and they were really of much greater importance than their names and purposes implied, for with the dinner went serious scientific talk.

So serious-minded was the Saturday Club that under the influence of Sir Joseph Banks it turned itself into nothing less than an African Association, by means of the following grandiloquent resolution:

That as no species of information is more ardently desired, or more generally useful, than that which improves the science of Geography; and as the vast Continent of Africa, notwithstanding the efforts of the Ancients, and the wishes of the Moderns, is still in a great measure unexplored, the Members of the Club do form themselves into an Association for

The Saturday Club gets down to work.

Promoting the Discovery of the Inland Parts of that Quarter of the World.

The African Association created an entirely new situation in the world of exploration: would-be explorers applied to this purely private institution financed by rich men and, if approved, were sent out as hired employees.

Soon after the formation of the association the flamboyant John Ledyard of Connecticut called on Sir Joseph Banks. John Ledyard, you remember, was the man who had urged President Jefferson to send an expedition to open up an overland route to California (see page 64).

Ledyard was an extraordinary person, all enthusiasm and little stability. He, like Banks, had also sailed with Captain Cook, though on the third voyage, not the first, and it was on that voyage that he had become so impressed with the potential wealth of California. Later, failing to find anyone who would pay him to do something spectacular in the way of exploration in his own country, he crossed to Europe and started on an incredible journey across Russia to the Pacific. He got as far as Siberia. "He says," reported President Jefferson, enjoying the joke, "that having no money, they kick him from place to place, and thus he expects to be kicked around the globe!" But in Siberia he was arrested and sent home by the zealous and unco-operative Russian police.

Ledyard at least had courage and undoubtedly possessed keenness and determination, and Sir Joseph Banks had believed in him and helped him in his Russian adventure. Now he turned up again: "Africa? Certainly! Where exactly would you like me to go?"

The African Association had been thinking about this. They had decided upon the western part of northern Africa, between the Sahara desert and the southern coast of the continent's great western bulge. Hereabouts lay Timbuctoo; and here, somewhere, flowed the great Niger river, though no one seemed to know the whereabouts of its mouth or its source, or in which direction it flowed. One of the authorities consulted by the association in preparation for the expedition was the work of Leo Africanus, a Moor of the fifteenth century, for it was thought that there must still be considerable Moorish, or Mohammedan, influence in this part of Africa.

Ledyard, when asked how soon he would be able to start, replied characteristically, "Tomorrow morning." Actually he sailed within three weeks. He found time to write home ecstatically to his mother: "I have tramped the world under my feet, laughed at fear, derided danger. Through millions of fierce savages, over parching deserts, the freezing north, the everlasting ice, and stormy seas have I passed without harm. How good is my God! What rich subjects I have for praise, love and admiration."

It was true; so far he had passed unscathed. But when he reached Cairo Ledyard succumbed, tragically and unnecessarily, to a self-administered dose of vitriol, which he had taken to cure a minor ailment. Certainly John Ledyard never did things by halves. And certainly he deserved a better fate.

The African Association had already fitted a second string to its bow. Mr Simon Lucas, more staid in character than Ledyard, had been shipped off to Tripoli with instructions to strike due south across the desert. But Lucas proved to have little resilience. Finding that inter-tribal wars were in progress, and failing to attach himself to any trading caravan, he gave up. He had penetrated only a very short distance into the desert.

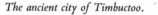

The ancient city of Timbuctoo.

The African Association had, however, gained something. Both their men had sent back useful information about North Africa. The position, before only guessed at but now more fully understood, was that Mohammedanism was still a very considerable power in North Africa. The African Arabs, the Berbers, sometimes loosely called the Moors, ruled the country. Most of the petty princes, whether of Arab blood or of one of the many black or near-black races, were of the Moslem religion, and all Moslems, by tradition, hated all Christians. There was much talk at this time, following discoveries in the Pacific, of the noble savage, an individual who would usually be on your side if you treated him aright. But it was plain that the noble savage did not exist in North Africa: the typical man of these parts had long ago graduated beyond the savage state; and, whether or not he was noble, he was likely to be deeply hostile.

In 1789 a certain Moorish merchant called Shabeni was telling people in London of the enormous wealth to be found by those who penetrated southwards across the Sahara. "We have heard of a city called Timbuctoo," wrote one of the association's founder members enthusiastically, "where gold is so plentiful as to adorn even the slaves; if we could get our manufactures into that country we should soon have gold enough." Here was the old El Dorado spirit cropping up again!

The next candidate to come before the African Association was Daniel Houghton, a retired Irish major who possessed a knowledge of the African coast where the minor, but still very considerable, river Gambia pours into the sea. Major Houghton was commissioned to penetrate northwards from the coast and to find both Timbuctoo and the river Niger.

Houghton's attempt was another tragic failure. He followed the Gambia river and then struck overland, encountering delays and difficulties from warring and predatory chiefs. When he had travelled more than halfway to Timbuctoo he was struck down by dysentery and died. He had met two of the misfortunes that were always to dog the footsteps of African explorers: the levy of extortionate tolls by local tribal kings, and the dreadful incidence of disease. Africa was not going to be kind to the white man.

Houghton had penetrated further than anyone before him. Moreover, he had learned that Timbuctoo lay on the Niger river and that that great river flowed eastwards (not westwards as had been suspected) between the Sahara and Africa's south-facing coast. A Scotsman with the strange and memorable name of Mungo Park* followed in Houghton's footsteps and reaped the benefit of his work.

Mungo was one of the thirteen children of a hard-working farmer of Selkirk in the Scottish lowlands. He was first apprenticed to a local doctor and then, with the encouragement of his brother-in-law (a protégé of Sir Joseph Banks) made his way to Edinburgh university where eventually he took his medical degree. He was then twenty-three years old, tall, handsome, ambitious and greatly interested in botany and zoology. He came to London to seek his fortune, and his brother-in-law introduced him to Sir Joseph Banks.

Banks got him a job as surgeon on an East India Company's ship, an ideal post in which a man who was an aspiring naturalist might increase his knowledge. Mungo Park took advantage of it and established a reputation in this field. In July 1794, he applied to Sir

*Mungo, however, is a perfectly authentic Celtic name; it means lovable or beloved.

In some villages Mungo Park learnt to appreciate the humanity of the black man.

Joseph Banks for the job that Houghton's death had left open. He got it.

Mungo Park's portrait shows a handsome young man, with wide-set honest eyes, finely chiselled nose and determined chin. Such a man would always do his duty. He might not prove an easy companion—London society later found him disappointingly taciturn—but his determination would be unshakeable. The African Association was fortunate in its choice.

After some irritating delay Mungo Park set out alone up the river Gambia and soon reached the trading post of Pisania. There he was advised to wait until the rainy season had passed, and wait he did, for five months, learning the local language. Here he met

Moorish slave-traders coming down from the interior. They proved unhelpful, as taciturn as himself. In the last month of 1795—while those left behind him in Europe watched apprehensively the course of the war against revolutionary France—Mungo Park finally set out on his exploration.

He took two black men with him as interpreters and servants; four more elected to go with him. He struck out towards the land of the Berbers and, perhaps foolishly, he scorned to wear Moorish clothes.

The first two black kings he met treated him well, though the second needed rather a heavy sweetening with presents. His wives teased Mungo for his colour—had he been dipped in milk as a baby? And that nose, surely it had been pinched each day by his mother to produce such a horrid malformation! Here was a new way of looking at the relative beauty of blacks and whites. Unaware of the horrid reversal of fortune that was awaiting him, Mungo said goodbye to these disconcerting but kindly ladies, and pushed on.

The first of his troubles came when horsemen charged down on him and accused him of trying to get through their master's country without paying. He only got away by surrendering half his trading goods. Soon after the process was repeated, with the same results.

Then came a pleasant interlude: when they reached the birthplace of one of his black companions they were regaled with two days of solid feasting. Mungo, learning rapidly to appreciate the humanity of the black man—which is more than some of those at home ever did—was profoundly affected by the tenderness of the mother's welcome for her long-lost son.

The son stayed behind; the other three self-appointed companions had already left. Mungo now had only his two servants.

The country through which he wished to pass was at war, and he was told that if he went that way he would certainly be taken for a spy. The only alternative was to make a detour northwards, and that would bring him into the Sahara desert and into the territory of the Christian-hating Moors. Mungo decided to make for the desert.

When he arrived at Benowm, the stronghold of an arrogant Moorish chief called Ali, he was peremptorily summoned to show himself before the chief's wife Fatima, who had never seen a white man and wanted to view one. He went, and after many insults was clapped into prison. Mungo found himself incarcerated in a squalid hut, with a hog tethered beside him, while from the open door the population jeered at the intentionally degrading spectacle. "From sunrise to sunset," he later wrote, "I was obliged to suffer with an unruffled countenance the insults of the rudest savages on earth."

Too well-guarded for escape, Mungo, as day followed day, received no clue as to his fate. There was a rumour that his eyes were to be taken out, for Ali did not like them and thought they resembled cats' eyes. Then at last something happened: he was taken out of his hut and forced to follow Ali on the warpath into the desert. His condition worsened, for he suffered like the rest from the heat and sandstorms, but in addition he was starved and could get no water except by begging it from the slaves or competing with the cattle. Fatima eventually had some compassion on him, and he found himself back in the camp at the desert's edge, where he had first been imprisoned.

He determined to try to escape as soon as the first rains came. Only one of his black companions was now left to him, and this one, Johnson, dared not face the risk of capture. He had his horse, though by now it was reduced to a scarecrow, and—by a stroke of luck, because Ali had been afraid of it—his pocket compass. His plans were hastened by the sinister news that he was going to be brought again into King Ali's presence. It was now or never. Here is Mungo Park's own description of the escape. Reflect that this is no made-up story, but cold, sober, terrifying reality.

About daybreak, Johnson, who had been listening to the Moors all night, came and whispered to me that they were asleep. The awful crisis was now arrived, when I was again either to taste the blessing of freedom, or languish out my days in captivity. A cold sweat moistened my forehead, as I thought on the dreadful alternative, and reflected that, one way or the other, my fate must be decided in the course of the ensuing day. But to deliberate was to lose the only chance of escaping. So, taking up my bundle, I stepped gently over the Negroes, who were sleeping in the open air, and having mounted my horse, I bade Johnson farewell, desiring him to take particular care of the papers I had entrusted him with, and inform my friends in Gambia that he had left me in good health, on my way to Bambara.

I proceeded with great caution; surveying each bush, and frequently listening and looking behind me for the Moorish horsemen, until I was about a mile from the town, when I was surprised to find myself in the neighbourhood of a korree [watering-place for cattle] belonging to the Moors. The shepherds followed me for about a mile, hooting and throwing stones after me; and when I was out of their reach, and had begun to indulge the pleasing hopes of escaping, I was again greatly alarmed to hear somebody holla behind me; and looking back, I saw three Moors on horseback, coming after me at full speed; whooping and brandishing their double-barrelled guns. I knew it was in vain to think of escaping, and therefore turned back and met them: when two of them caught hold of my bridle, one on

each side, and the third, presenting his musket, told me I must go back to Ali. When the human mind has for some time been fluctuating between hope and despair, tortured with anxiety, and hurried from one extreme to another, it affords a sort of gloomy relief to know the worst that can possibly happen: such was my situation. An indifference about life, and all its enjoyments, had completely benumbed my faculties, and I rode back with the Moors with apparent unconcern.

Then something that must have seemed like a miracle happened. The three Moors ransacked his bundle and took out his cloak, the only thing worth having: they were nothing more than common robbers and their references to King Ali had been pure bluff. For a while Mungo pleaded desperately for his cloak, and then he realized the true position. He watched the Moors depart out of sight, and struck into the woods for safety: "It is impossible to describe the joy that arose in my mind, when I looked around and concluded I was out of danger. I felt like one recovered from sickness; I breathed freer; I found unusual lightness in my limbs; even the desert looked pleasant. . . ." How fortunate he was—in the wilds of Africa, with no food, no water, no companions, and no cloak!

He pushed on and on in search of a native village or a watering-place. He climbed a tree, to survey only "a dismal uniformity of shrubs and sand". Utterly exhausted and feeling he was at the point of death, he lay down and lost consciousness. In the cool of the evening he recovered a little and summoned all his resolution to make one more effort. He plodded on, driving his horse before him. Darkness began to fall. Clouds loomed up, and his spirits rose, for surely rain would fall. But it was a sandstorm. Again he pushed on; and then at last came drops of rain, and then a deluge. He assuaged his thirst by sucking his wet clothes and wringing water from them.

Through the night Mungo travelled on. Suddenly his horse started and, looking round, Mungo saw a light through the trees, and then more lights. A native village? But there were no signs of cultivation. A Moorish encampment then? Mungo was torn between dread of the Moors and the desire to find the oasis or water-hole that must be somewhere near. By luck he found the water-hole before running into the Moors, though it was a near thing when a woman saw him and screamed. Then at the water-hole the croaking of frogs so frightened his horse that he was obliged to keep them quiet by beating the water with a branch while the animal drank. Day was dawning, and from the top of a tree Mungo Park surveyed the land. He discovered a native village in the distance. By noon he had managed to reach it. The headman refused him food or succour, but a poor woman in a hut outside the wall was kinder.

So did Mungo Park escape death by the narrowest margin. For two more days his position was precarious. But then he fell in

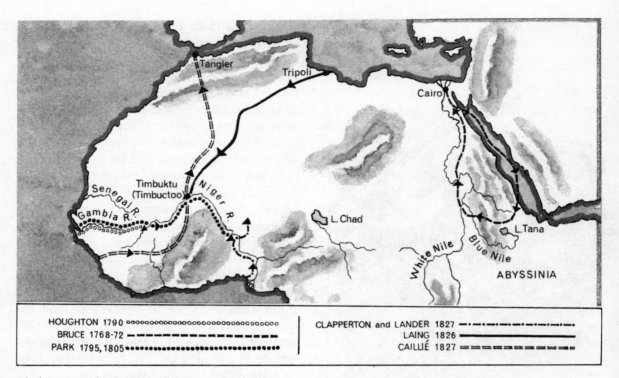

The beginnings of European exploration in North Africa.

with a friendly party of refugees who had fled from the fighting and together they came into the fertile and friendly country of Bambara. After about a fortnight's travelling one of the party called out, "See, the water!"

Looking forwards, I saw with infinite pleasure the object of my mission—the long sought for, majestic Niger, glittering to the morning sun, as broad as the Thames at Westminster, and flowing slowly to the eastward. I hastened to the brink and, having drunk of the water, lifted up my fervent thanks in prayer to the Great Ruler of all things for having thus far crowned my endeavours with success.

If any explorer ever deserved his moment of success it was Mungo Park. Soon he learnt that Timbuctoo, on that same river, was in the hands of those merciless fanatics the Moors. Then he realized that to follow the river he had

to have a canoe, which he did not possess and could not hire or buy. To persevere further in these conditions would only be to throw away his life, so Mungo Park turned back reluctantly for home. The journey back was supremely difficult. But he managed it.

Mungo Park returned to England in 1797, to the acclaim of the Royal Geographical Society in particular and of London society in general. He does not seem to have appreciated social flattery. He wrote his *Travels*, which has since become a classic, and then he returned to Scotland, to marry and to settle down to life as a country doctor.

But he could not settle. Very few of those who explored in Africa could settle: the continent, if it did not kill them, captivated them. Mungo Park was also goaded on by the enthusiasm of Sir Joseph Banks and his friends,

82

the industrialists, the scientists, the politicians, the enthusiasts and the philanthropists of Great Britain.

In 1805 he found himself at the head of a military expedition to explore the Niger. One cannot help feeling that he would have been better off on his own. The expedition consisted of two sailors, one military lieutenant and thirty-five volunteers from a regiment stationed at Goree on the west coast of Africa and reputed to be the dregs of the British army. The volunteers had been promised double pay and discharge on their return. But there was no discharge and no return. All of them died.

Mungo Park always drove himself to the limit of his endurance. He drove his followers in the same way, though he made superhuman efforts to combat difficulties and to save lives. But he never seriously contemplated turning back.

The expedition was to sail up the Gambia river, trek with pack animals across the 400 miles to the Niger river, and then travel by boat the length of that great river, past Timbuctoo and on to its mouth. They met every difficulty, from thieving and threatening natives to wild bees that stampeded their animals. But chiefly they suffered from rain, damp and disease. By the time they reached the Niger river there were only ten of them left. They hired a large canoe and set out. Mungo Park wrote home to his employer, the Colonial Secretary: "Though all the Europeans who are with me should die, and though I were myself half dead, I would still persevere; and if I could not succeed in the object of my mission, I would at least die on the Niger."

That is in fact what happened. There were no European survivors, and Mungo Park died on the river Niger. After a year's silence the sole

survivor, Park's servant, who had been sent back with letters, reached the coast. Timbuctoo had been reached, or at any rate passed, for only the town's port, Kabara, lies actually on the river. A further distance of nearly 1,000 miles had been traversed, and they had only another 600 miles to go to reach the coast. But at that point the increasing enmity of the local tribes had proved too much for the little party. A shooting match developed, not the first, between the men in the canoe and their enemies on the banks of the river. They came to a place of overhanging rock where the natives—the fierce and well-armed Tauregs—possessed an overwhelming advantage. Mungo Park and the surviving few took to the water. All were drowned.

Over twenty years were to elapse before a white man sailed down the Niger to its mouth or made known to the western world the secrets of Timbuctoo.

An English naval captain, Hugh Clapperton, and his servant Richard Lander, were responsible for the final exploration of the river. Major Alexander Laing, a Scotsman, and M. René Caillié, a Frenchman, were the first visitors to Timbuctoo. Theirs is a strange story of rivalry between nations.

Major Laing's adventures were mixed up with a romantic love affair. He planned to travel southwards from Tripoli. But before he set out he fell madly in love with the British consul's daughter there, and caused that official a great deal of anxiety by insisting on marrying the girl in the last two days before his departure. Miss Emma Warrington was one of those ethereal beauties beloved of nineteenth-century novelists. The gallant major sent her impassioned love-letters from the sandy wastes of the Sahara.

Another aspect of the brave romanticism of Major Laing was his utter refusal to approach the Moslem city of Timbuctoo in any other guise than that of a Christian soldier. On the way out he was treacherously attacked, wounded in over a dozen places, and left for dead. The attentions of his faithful servant saved his life, however, and soon he was writing to his wife with his left hand, explaining that he had hurt a finger—and suffering agonies of mind that when she saw him again she would find him disfigured.

Major Laing reached Timbuctoo in 1826, holding himself to be the first white man to do so. Openly he toured the city, asking many questions of the inhabitants so that he might send home a worthwhile report. He was allowed to leave. Then when he was two days' journey out he was murdered, probably as a suspected spy. Great efforts were made later to salvage his papers, but without success; it was widely rumoured that the French consul had gained possession of them. Emma Laing learnt eventually of her husband's death. She married someone else, and died of tuberculosis three years later. . . .

René Caillié was of lowlier origin, early orphaned, largely self-educated; at one time he had been an officer's servant, at one time a sailor. He was attracted by the 10,000 francs offered by the Geographical Society of Paris to the first Frenchman to reach and report on Timbuctoo. But he was also a brave man, less romantic than Laing but equally determined. He learnt Arabic, and had the good sense to disguise himself as an Arab while he was making the journey.

He approached Timbuctoo from the west coast, as Mungo Park had done, though he did not use the Niger river. He often received bad treatment from the slave-traders with whom he travelled; but he was undoubtedly helped by his disguise. In 1828, when he was twenty-eight, and after a year's travelling and a long bout of scurvy, he reached Timbuctoo. He stayed there a fortnight. In order that there should be no suspicion that he had in fact not made the journey, he elected to return not by the way he had come but north, across the desert, to Tangier. Again he met with ill-treatment and at the very end only narrowly escaped death. But he won his 10,000 francs and great renown.

In England, however, the news of his achievement was unkindly received. This Frenchman from the gutter! He had not even had the courage, not to say the common decency, to travel as a Christian soldier, as had Major Laing. He was even accused, ridiculously, of never having been to Timbuctoo: somehow he had just got hold of and used Major Laing's missing papers.

In 1848 the British Foreign Office employed a German, Heinrich Barth, to explore in the Timbuctoo and lake Chad area, and Barth produced a valuable report which helped to rehabilitate Caillié in British eyes. It was a little late in the day. Caillié had been dead ten years. Sometimes explorers are ill served by those whose knowledge and understanding of the world they seek to increase.

And Timbuctoo itself? Both Laing and Caillié found it a most disappointing place, "presenting a monotonous and barren scene" and already in decay. Much of the glory it undoubtedly had in the times of Moslem greatness had already departed.

But at least it now had a definite place on the map, and the excitement of international rivalry had helped to make it a household word. Bishops could make rhymes about it, and little Victorian boys and girls could tell each other to go there.

David Livingstone (1813–73).

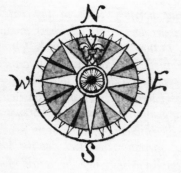

CHAPTER 8

Light on the darkness of Africa

THE explorer David Livingstone was a man from whom loving-kindness came forth as naturally as scent from a flower, a man in whose presence other men felt better. He wrote of Africa: "The strangest disease I have seen in this country seems really to be broken-heartedness, and it attacks free men who have been captured and made slaves." To the healing of this broken-heartedness he devoted himself for more than thirty years. He loved the black African, and towards the end of his life, after the death of his wife, he looked on Africa as his home.

David Livingstone was born in 1813. He was another determined young Scotsman like Mungo Park, who saw to it that he got the sort of education he needed. He was another

87

young doctor pulling himself up by his shoe-strings, a graduate of Glasgow after spending his youth in a cotton mill. It was not easy to do this sort of thing: David was twenty-seven years old by the time that he was a qualified doctor.

From the start his intention had been to become a medical missionary. He had hoped to go to China, but war made this impossible. Then in 1840 he met Robert Moffat, like himself a servant of the London Missionary Society;* and before the year was out he was travelling to Cape Town to join him.

Moffat's base was at Kuruman, in Bechuana-land. Livingstone was given the job of prospecting outwards for the setting-up of new stations, and he took to the task with enthusiasm. Soon indeed he was taking on jobs that were not strictly part of the curriculum—such as relieving a frightened village from a plague of lions that were destroying their cattle. That job left its mark on him—literally.

With his friend and first convert, Mebalwe, he set out on this task. A lion appeared. Mebalwe fired and missed, and the animal got away through the circle of beaters. So did two more. Disappointed, Livingstone began to retrace his steps. Then another lion appeared, and Livingstone emptied both his barrels into it. With cries of "He is shot!" the beaters began to run towards the lion. Livingstone, however, saw that the lion's tail was erect in anger and shouted to them to let him reload and fire again.

When in the act of ramming down the bullets I heard a shout. Starting, and looking half-round, I saw the lion just in the act of springing upon me. I was upon a little height; he caught my shoulder as he sprang, and we both came to the ground below to-gether. Growling horribly close to my ear, he shook me as a terrier does a rat. The shock produced a stupor similar to that which seems to be felt by a mouse after the first shake of the cat. It caused a sort of dreaminess, in which there was no sense of pain nor feeling of terror, though quite conscious of all that was happening. It was like what patients partially under the influence of chloroform describe, who see all the operation, but feel not the knife. This singular condition was not the result of any mental process. The shake annihilated fear, and allowed no sense of horror in looking round at the beast. This peculiar state is probably produced in all animals killed by the carnivora; and if so, is a merciful provision by our benevolent Creator for lessening the pain of death. Turning round to relieve myself of the weight, as he had one paw on the back of my head, I saw his eyes directed to Mebalwe, who was trying to shoot him at a distance of ten or fifteen yards. His gun, a flint one, missed fire in both barrels; the lion immediately left me, and, attacking Mebalwe, bit his thigh. Another man, whose life I had saved before, after he had been tossed by a buffalo, attempted to spear the lion while he was biting Mebalwe. He left Mebalwe and caught this man by the shoulder, but at that moment the bullets he had received took effect, and he fell down dead. . . . Besides crunching the bone into splinters, he left eleven teeth wounds in the upper part of my arm.

Livingstone felt that he had been lucky. He had on a tartan jacket, which, he thought, cleaned the lion's teeth before they entered his flesh. He suffered only the inconvenience of having a false joint in his limb, whilst poor Mebalwe's wound kept on breaking out even a year later. When asked by solemn persons in later days what·he thought of while the lion stood over him he was inclined to reply, "I

---

*Founded in 1795 as an undenominational organization for overseas missionary work.

was thinking what part of me he would eat first." Livingstone did not believe in heroics.

He now had his own missionary station and was married to Moffat's daughter. He managed to convert and to win the friendship of the local chief. To the north lay the barrier of the Kalahari desert. Why, asked the chief, were not the people beyond the Kalahari told the good Christian news? But no, he added at once, of course the barrier was too great.

That was a challenge. In 1848 Livingstone wrote: "All my desires tend forwards, to the north. . . . Why, we have a world before us here. We have no missionary beyond this—all is dark." By 1849 he had set out across the Kalahari. With him were two friends who were big-game hunters and, travelling in a covered wagon, his wife and their young children.

They crossed the desert and were the first to discover lake Ngami. But the enmity of a local chief and his refusal to let them pass—a recurring difficulty in all African exploration —sent them back to their base. In the next year's expedition another African menace, the tsetse fly, death to horse and oxen, defeated them. In the third effort in 1851 thirst nearly defeated them, but not quite. They reached Linyanti, capital of the Makololo tribe, and with the friendly help of these people they pushed on and struck the Zambesi river.

This piece of successful exploration was important for two reasons. In the first place Livingstone found that the Zambesi flowed in the centre of the continent, where the maps showed that it did not.

Secondly, this discovery gave him an idea: the Zambesi river was perhaps a highway by which the missionary and the trader might penetrate the centre of Africa from either coast.

From that time onwards Livingstone was essentially the explorer, though his driving force was always missionary and humanitarian. As he explored further north and came more and more in contact with the slave-trade he became convinced that Christianity must go hand in hand with commerce. He felt that there was only one effective way of combating the slave-trade and that was to drive it out by *legitimate* trade. Africa thirsted after European goods. Let those goods be offered them, but in exchange for ivory and other natural products and not in exchange for human bodies and souls.

Livingstone had the sense to stop carrying his family about with him. He took them all the way down to the Cape, saw them off to England, and retraced his steps. He was about to set out on his first major piece of exploration, a four-year effort in which he was to travel from coast to coast, discover the Victoria falls and, more than once, nearly die of fever.

Back with the Makololo tribe, Livingstone was given a liberal supply of porters by the admiring chief. These native porters seem to have enlisted with great willingness: they were Livingstone's friends, and he was their father.

Up the Zambesi they went and for a long while all was well. Livingstone was overjoyed by the beauty of the river, which at times even reminded him of his native Clyde. Then they approached the slaving area and difficulties increased. The native chiefs were more suspicious,

The Victoria falls, on the Zambesi.

more demanding. There were delays, a too-quick depletion of precious trade goods and very real hunger. For a while there was nothing to eat but a sort of porridge made from the manioc root—Livingstone said it was like starch made from diseased potatoes.

They found, to their disappointment, that the river Zambesi was petering out. They proceeded by land, struggling through the damp forest and against the effects of fever. They crossed two tributaries of the Congo river and eventually came to signs of civilization in Portuguese Angola. At last they saw the line of the sea. The Makololos were amazed. "We marched along with our father," they said, "believing that what the ancients had always told us was true, that the world has no end; but all at once the world said to us, 'I am finished; there is no more of me!'"

All of them received great help and kindness from the Portuguese and also from a British naval unit which was present on an anti-slave-trade patrol. Livingstone was nursed back to health and then offered a passage home. It must have been a great temptation. But he said he must take his Makololo porters back to their tribe —and he did.

Then, reluctantly realizing that there was no easy trade route from the western coast to the centre, Livingstone turned his attention to the east. His friend, the chief, warned him that to the east the Zambesi ran down through many rapids. At first, therefore, he did not follow the river but made his way across beautiful country filled with game: "hundreds of buffaloes and zebras grazed on the open spaces, and there stood lordly elephants, moving nothing apparently but the proboscis". Livingstone's reaction was for his times highly unusual; he wished he had a camera so that he could photograph the scene before men's rifles made it a thing of the past.

Then he heard of *Mosi-oa-tunya*, which means "smoke does sound there". This was the name of a waterfall, whose crashing waters sent out clouds of spray. Livingstone was the first white man to visit it, and he called it the Victoria falls, in honour of his queen.

He made a thorough inspection. "When about half a mile from the falls, I left the canoe by which we had come down thus far and embarked in a lighter one, with men well acquainted with the rapids." That the men possessed such knowledge was just as well, for Livingstone induced them to land him on an island on the very edge of the falls. "Creeping with awe to the verge, I peered down," he wrote. Below him a 1,000-yard breadth of water cascaded down for 100 feet and then was compressed into a narrow channel down which a further cataract roared. From it rose a white vapour, which at a height of 200 or 300 feet turned into a dark cloud and then fell down in the form of a constant shower. And at the edge of this shower Livingstone planted coffee beans and peach and apricot stones, and then cut his initials and the date on a tree: D.L. 1855. "This was the only instance in which I indulged in this piece of vanity."

A year after leaving the Makololo chief, Livingstone reached the eastern coast and, again, the help and welcome of the Portuguese. He believed that this route he had pioneered to the sea was, in spite of the Zambesi's falls and rapids, a feasible one. He returned, at last, to England. News of his exploits had preceded him, and he found himself a famous man.

Meanwhile Richard Francis Burton had been turning *his* attention to Africa.

Burton, eight years younger than Livingstone, was an English aristocrat, an Oxford scholar, an army officer, a linguist, and an enthusiastic Arabist. He was a lover of everything Arabian,

Richard Francis Burton (1821–90).

but despised the black African. His incentive to travel and explore was certainly not missionary zeal, neither was it love of gain, nor even obedience to the orders of an ambitious government. At the lowest it could be called pure restlessness; at the highest, pure love of exploration, the desire to overcome nature, to learn and to know. In 1853 he made—in disguise—a romantic dash to the Moslems' holy and forbidden city of Mecca. Then the following year, while still an army officer, he obtained permission to explore the African coast of the Persian gulf. He took with him a fellow officer, traveller and big-game hunter, John Speke. Not many years later, the two devoutly wished that they had never met. As Alan Moorehead puts it in his book *The White Nile*, to which the following account is much indebted, "Burton needed a disciple and instead he got a rival."

Their first effort ended in disaster, almost before they got under way. They were attacked by Somali tribesmen, both men were wounded and Speke was carried off a prisoner. He managed to escape, but he laid the blame of the whole episode on Burton's provocative behaviour, and naturally he was not pleased. Burton, meanwhile, impatient of delays, had taken the opportunity to visit another forbidden city, the Somali town of Harar, now in Ethiopia.

After the Crimean war the two met again and joined forces on another expedition. It was sponsored by the British Foreign Office and the Royal Geographical Society* and was backed with hard cash to the amount of £1,000. Its aim was the discovery of the source of the Nile, the whereabouts of the great lakes and their relation to the river.

The two men elected to set out from the island of Zanzibar, a great slaving depot off the east coast of Africa, some six degrees south of the equator. Burton liked the place, for it was Moslem and largely Arabian. But Speke found it dirty; and it gave Burton his first bout of malaria.

At length they got away and struck due west. Progress was slow, as ever in Africa: porters preferred to dance through the night rather than march through the day; there was long haggling with local chiefs before the expedition could pass through their territories. Both Burton and Speke were ill. Neither grew any fonder of the other.

At the end of eight months they reached the shores of lake Tanganyika. After a first disappointing glimpse, Burton was enraptured by its beauty; Speke, suffering from eye trouble, could hardly see it.

And then came a rather surprising develop-

---

*Founded in 1830 for the purpose of furthering exploration.

ment, which was to cause much trouble. After they had retired to the nearest slave-trading base, Speke struck up north on his own. Burton said he had sent him as his subordinate; Speke said he had taken over because Burton was so ill. Speke discovered the great lake Nyanza which, in Livingstone's fashion, he named Victoria Nyanza after his queen. He had in fact discovered the source of the Nile.

He claimed as much. But he had only intuition and local stories to support his claim. He surveyed only a tiny portion of the southern shores of the huge lake, and his statement that the Nile made its exit from the northern part of the lake was guesswork. Speke was of course aware of this. He went back to England ahead of Burton, who was still ill, and Burton felt that he was seeking undue publicity and praise. He was hardly appeased when a fresh expedition was arranged for Speke, from which he was excluded.

Speke and his assistant James Grant, an efficient but also a self-effacing and most amenable character, set off in 1860, again from Zanzibar. At first they travelled north-westwards, and then northwards by the western shores of lake Victoria Nyanza. In the lake area the explorers came upon very powerful tribes, whose cruel and highly autocratic monarchs detained them and made great demands on them.

When he had reached a latitude a little north of the northern shore of the lake, Speke turned eastwards, hoping thus to strike the Nile and to follow it upstream to the lake. This, in fact, was what he did. With great excitement and a full heart he saw the river issuing from the lake in spectacular falls, which he named the Ripon falls after the president of the Royal Geographical Society. He came home, now entirely convinced that he had discovered the source of the Nile.

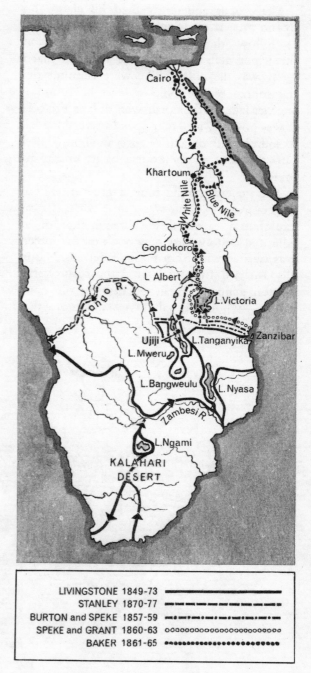

LIVINGSTONE 1849-73
STANLEY 1870-77
BURTON and SPEKE 1857-59
SPEKE and GRANT 1860-63
BAKER 1861-65

Explorations in Central Africa.

93

Many geographers accepted his claim, but by no means all. Speke had not been able to follow the river that proceeded from the Ripon falls far enough to establish that it really was the Nile. There were rumours that the source of the Nile was to be found in another lake, to the north-west of lake Victoria. It was possible, too, that Speke's river Nile had its source south of lake Victoria and poured itself into that lake in the course of its northward journey.

The general public took a great interest in the controversy. This was a time when African exploration captured the imagination of all educated Britons: any new book on the subject was awaited with tremendous eagerness. Naturally Richard Burton entered the controversy. Burton genuinely believed that his old companion—whom he half loved and more than

half hated—was wrong. And Burton had a powerful pen and a supple tongue.

In 1864 Burton and Speke were booked to confront one another on a public platform in Bath at the annual meeting of the British Association for the Advancement of Science. It was believed that Speke dreaded this confrontation. The meeting began, but Speke did not appear. While Burton and others waited on the platform a note was handed up. Its contents were whispered to Burton. Speke had met with a fatal accident from his own gun while out shooting. Burton staggered, sat down, and cried, "My God, he's killed himself!" Then he pulled himself together and managed to give a lecture on another subject.

Had Speke killed himself? We shall never know and we must not assume that he had. The verdict was accidental death. Perhaps a less

worried Speke would not have had an accident with his gun. In any event it was a tragic and unnecessary end to the career of a brilliant explorer.

The Nile controversy, however, was by no means ended. For the continuance of the story we must meet yet another explorer, Samuel White Baker.

Baker was a splendid figure, physically powerful, courageous and practical, good at getting his way and almost as good as Livingstone at getting on with natives. He was everyone's ideal of an explorer, and, since he travelled with a young and beautiful wife as courageous as himself, he was also everyone's romantic ideal.

In 1863 Baker and his wife travelled up the Nile from Khartoum to the slave-trading post of Gondokoro, intending to search for Speke and Grant, of whom nothing had been heard for over two years. Shortly afterwards the two explorers themselves arrived in Gondokoro on their way back from lake Victoria Nyanza. Baker had had his own ambitions about finding the true source of the Nile, but when Speke and Grant told him of their exploits he was pretty well convinced that the job had been done. This meeting, therefore, while a most happy one for the exhausted explorers of lake Victoria, was something of a disappointment for Baker. But Speke was generous and told Baker of another large lake he had heard of in the area, to the north-west of Victoria. The discovery of this was offered to him as a sort of consolation prize: perhaps at least the Nile flowed *through* it.

So, while Speke went back to England, Baker went on to find this other lake, which is now known as lake Albert. He found that the Nile did indeed pass through its waters.

Baker's discovery, in fact, further complicated the Nile controversy. If the Nile flowed through lake Albert, was this lake to be regarded as a secondary source of the great river, or was it perhaps its primary source? Perhaps the real Nile entered lake Albert at its southern end? Perhaps it started even further south—perhaps even in lake Tanganyika? The Royal Geographical Society felt that a serious attempt should be made to clear up this problem of the source of the Nile and the relationship of the river to Africa's lakes. In 1865 they asked David Livingstone to make this attempt.

In the past ten years, Livingstone had managed to impress those in authority with the urgency of the need to open up Africa, so that Christianity and commerce might benefit its peoples and save them from the ever-increasing demoralization of the slave-trade. The outcome

Samuel White Baker (1821–93) and his wife.

of this—a triumph for his powers of persuasion—had been his appointment in 1858 as the leader of a government-sponsored Zambesi expedition of imposing size.

It was a disappointing expedition. It so often seems that an explorer fares better on his own. The steamboats provided were rotten; some of Livingstone's white subordinates were far from helpful, particularly his younger brother, who was a trouble-maker; and in the course of this expedition his wife, who had come out to Africa to help him, died of a fever. One new discovery was made: this was lake Nyasa, the most southerly of the great lakes. Livingstone envisaged it patrolled by steamboats, monitoring and finally defeating the slave-traders.

He returned to England in 1864. His reputation was still so high that he was the obvious choice for the leadership of the expedition proposed by the Royal Geographical Society to settle once and for all the great disputes over the watersheds of central Africa.

Livingstone elected to set out from Zanzibar, though he disliked the place no less than Speke had done. He said it ought to be called Stinkibar not Zanzibar, and he watched with horror the way in which the slaves in the market were examined like so many animals and made to show their paces in running to retrieve a stick.

Livingstone had two particular problems to solve. The first was to establish the source of the Nile—he himself favoured a more southerly source than Speke's lake Victoria. The second was to establish the course of the Congo river, whose tributaries he had crossed in his earlier explorations to the west coast.

He struck westwards round the southern end of lake Nyasa and, after many delays caused by local wars and recurrent bouts of fever, discovered lake Bangweulu. Eventually he made his way back to the eastern shores of lake Tanganyika and to the slave-trade depot of Ujiji, which was in touch with the coast. Livingstone had arranged for stores to be sent to Ujiji: through the desertion of a porter he had lost his medicine chest, and he hoped that his report of the loss would have got through to the coast and that a replacement would now be waiting for him. He found neither stores nor medicine. He knew this was serious—later it was seen to have been virtually his death sentence. But he took the blow with his usual patience and philosophy and carried on. It was already three years since he had left Zanzibar.

In May 1871 he reached a large native village called Nyangwe. It was on the river Lualaba, which Livingstone thought might be the upper reaches of the Nile and which was, in fact, the upper reaches of the Congo. There he witnessed a terrible massacre instigated by the slavers in their ruthless hunt for slaves. Sickened, Livingstone wrote an impassioned account of it. He returned to Ujiji, where again he was disappointed in his expectation of replenishments awaiting him. Again he was ill.

People at home were growing a little worried at lack of news of him. Well they might be. But then David Livingstone was very much a law unto himself—the independent and unpredictable traveller. He was probably all right. An expedition did set out, and then returned when some news filtered through that he was still alive. Burton, who often showed his worst side in his letters, voiced the feeling of some when he said it was rather *infra dig* to have to go out and discover a "mish" (missionary).

But there was at least one man who thought otherwise. His name was Stanley.

Henry Morton Stanley was an unlikely person to put cynical and hard-bitten people to shame. He was a tough and hard-bitten man himself. A Welshman by birth and an American

by citizenship, he had become a successful and adventurous journalist on the somewhat sensational American newspaper, the *New York Herald*. In 1871 he got himself the assignment of finding Livingstone, hoping for a scoop.

As everyone knows, Stanley made his scoop. But we must be fair to him, which is more than some contemporary Englishmen were. His famous greeting, made when he at last reached the great explorer at Ujiji, was neither a tasteless joke made for effect nor a cold salutation made from insensitivity. Far from it. The only effect Stanley sought was to hide his own excess of feeling. Here is his description of the meeting:

My heart beats fast, but I must not let my face betray my emotions, lest it shall detract from the dignity of a white man appearing under such extraordinary circumstances.

So I did that which I thought was most dignified, I pushed back the crowds, and, passing from the rear, walked down a living avenue of people, until I came in front of the semicircle of Arabs, in the front of which stood the white man with the grey beard. As I advanced slowly towards him I noticed he was pale, looked wearied, had a grey beard, wore a bluish cap with a faded gold band round it, had on a red-sleeved waistcoat, and a pair of grey tweed trousers. I would have run to him, only I was a coward in the presence of such a mob—would have embraced him, only, he being an Englishman, I did not know how he would receive me; so I did what cowardice and false pride suggested was the best thing—walked deliberately to him, took off my hat, and said:

"Dr Livingstone, I presume?"

"Yes," said he, with a kind smile, lifting his cap slightly.

I replace my hat on my head, and he puts on his cap, and we both grasp hands, and I then say aloud:

"I thank God, Doctor, I have been permitted to see you."

He answered, *"I feel thankful that I am here to welcome you."*

Stanley's admiration for Livingstone was genuine and unbounded. Soon he was a disciple at the feet of the sage. These two, the brash journalist and the Christian missionary, the young man from the New World at the start of his career and the old man from the Old World at the end of his, assumed with ease an understanding friendship.

Livingstone recovered something of his health and the two went on an expedition by canoe up to the north of lake Tanganyika, where they disproved a theory of Burton's about the source of the Nile by showing that the lake had no outlet on the north. Then Stanley did his best to persuade Livingstone to come back to England with him. He failed. Taking the elder man's despatches and reports with him (including those on the massacre of the slaves) and promising to send more porters from the coast for Livingstone's further explorations, he said farewell.

The porters arrived in due course and Livingstone struck westwards, still in search of damning evidence against the slave-traders, still in search of the source of the Nile. That was in August 1872. On 30 April 1873, in the heart of Africa, Livingstone died. So great was the love of his native porters for him that they carried his body a nine months' journey to the coast, from where it was brought by cruiser to England.

Stanley was in America when he heard of the great explorer's death. He determined to go back to Africa and finish Livingstone's job.

This he did, though in his own way. "Each man has his own way," he wrote in his diary. "His [Livingstone's], I think, had its defects, though the old man, personally, has been almost Christlike for goodness, patience, and self-sacrifice. The selfish and wooden-headed world requires mastering, as well as loving charity." Stanley imposed ruthless discipline on his porters and sometimes treated them brutally if he considered it necessary. He was prepared to shoot his way through hostile tribes, and even to join in a native war so that he might get a chance of revenge upon a tribe that had thwarted him.

In 1874, the year after Livingstone's death, Stanley set out at the head of a large and well-found expedition that had three objectives: first, to sail all round lake Victoria in order to ascertain whether the river pouring out at Ripon falls entered the lake elsewhere; secondly, to sail round lake Tanganyika to prove or disprove any connection between that lake and the Nile; and thirdly, to follow Livingstone's river Lualaba to the sea.

All three objectives were carried out. Stanley proved that lake Victoria really was the source of the Nile; no other great streams left the lake and the streams entering it had no ascertainable connection with the river that went out at Ripon falls. He proved that lake Tanganyika had no outlet that could possibly be the Nile. He proved that the Lualaba became the Congo river and that, performing a great loop northwards, it turned westwards to empty itself into the Atlantic 1,000 miles or so down the coast from the mouth of Mungo Park's river Niger. Stanley was a great explorer and he performed his triple task as few others could have performed it. Nevertheless, when he finally reached the west coast, just short of 1,000 days from the beginning of his journey, he was a haggard wreck, and more than half his party had died on the way.

Africa—cruel but fascinating Africa, exacting but rewarding Africa—was now ripe for exploitation by the rival European powers, and Stanley took some part in that exploitation. He later received a knighthood. So did Richard Burton, for services to his country as consul in many lands. John Speke, who had been right about the source of the Nile, was accorded a commemorative plaque at Ripon falls and his father was given permission to add a crocodile and a hippopotamus to the family's coat of arms—an honour that may not have seemed quite so ludicrously inadequate in Victorian times.

As for Livingstone, he was given the honour of burial in Westminster Abbey. On his tomb is written:

For 30 years his life was spent in an unwearied effort to evangelize the native races, to explore the undiscovered secrets, to abolish the desolating slave-trade, of Central Africa, where with his last words he wrote: "All I can add in my solitude is may Heaven's rich blessing come down on everyone, American, English or Turk, who will help to heal this open sore of the world."

The writings and persuasiveness of David Livingstone contributed greatly to the healing of this open sore. Three years after his death the British government brought pressure to bear on Zanzibar, and the slave-market that had so appalled him was closed for good. The slave-trade had received its death blow, though for many years it lingered on in Arabia itself, in the Sudan and in far Timbuctoo.

So can an explorer, by his determination and powers of endurance, above all by his impassioned response to what he finds, not only contribute to world knowledge but also influence world history for its good.

CHAPTER 9

Cooper's creek

THE exploration of Africa ushered in an era of international rivalry, but in the exploration of Australia there was no more dangerous rivalry than that between two youthful states of a pacifically growing colony. In Africa explorers were concerned with a multiplicity of lakes and overpowering rivers; in Australia they were concerned with rivers that disappeared and a single large lake that existed only in their imaginations.

Australia was certainly different. As a land mass it is very ancient, and curiously isolated. When the world's mammals were evolving it became disconnected from the land mass of Asia and thereafter retained and developed its own distinctive and archaic species of mammal, the marsupial. Man, sometime in the last

1,000,000 years, came down to inhabit it, perhaps when access was easier than it is now, and remained isolated and undisturbed in a timeless Stone Age. Spaniards and Portuguese sailors sighted it in the sixteenth century; the Dutch and English inspected it in the seventeenth but they were not impressed and went away. Captain Cook made his more extensive discoveries towards the end of the eighteenth century. At about the same time England lost her American colonies and needed somewhere else to dump all those unfortunate minor malefactors whom she condemned to deportation. Her eyes turned to the new discovery. So in 1787 the first convict ship sailed to Botany Bay, and the white man's history in Australia began.

For some twenty years the white man was too busy settling down along the coast to think much of the interior. But naturally the interior intrigued him. The area was obviously vast—what did it contain? A certain aridity and lack of greenness around him made him dream of a large lake or a beautiful Mediterraneanlike inland sea.

The obvious thing to do was to find out—and young Australia did not lack the adventurous spirit. The first obstacle that had to be conquered was the range of high and rugged mountains that hemmed in the settlements along the south-east coast. Sheep-rearing had become a major industry, and in 1813 a drought made it urgently necessary to extend the area of grazing. Necessity is sometimes the mother of pioneering as well as of invention. Three men finally conquered the mountains, and found the sought-for pastures. Their names were Wentworth, Lawson and Blaxland.

Fifteen years later Charles Sturt, secretary to the governor of New South Wales, made two explorations and established how the only appreciable river system of the continent behaved—the Darling river running into the Murray and the Murray into the sea. He very much wanted to penetrate further into the interior but he had, unhappily, undermined his health by his efforts. In 1840 he watched his friend Edward Eyre start on the journey that he himself so much wanted to make. But Eyre, having penetrated 400 miles north of Adelaide, found the country so sullenly barren that he vowed he wanted nothing to do with it and angrily named the hill from which he finally viewed it as Mount Hopeless.

Sturt, on the other hand, still dreamed of a bright inland sea beyond the desert: "Let any man," he declared, "lay the map of Australia before him, and regard the blank upon its surface, and then let me ask him if it would not be an honourable achievement to be the first to place foot upon its centre." At last, in 1844, at the age of forty-nine but much improved in health, he set out for the interior. He and his

First explorations in Australia.

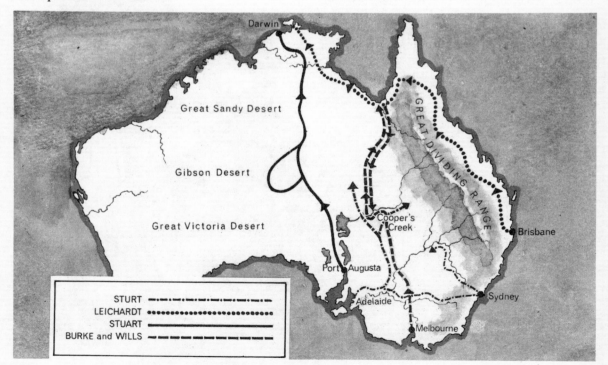

STURT —·—·—·—·—·—·—·—·—
LEICHARDT ●●●●●●●●●●●●●●●●●
STUART ▬▬▬▬▬▬▬▬▬
BURKE and WILLS ▬ ▬ ▬ ▬ ▬ ▬

sixteen companions and their flock of sheep were given a spectacular send-off.

Some way inland he set up an advanced base and pushed forward with a smaller party. He travelled through a silent, primeval emptiness where only the marsupial kangaroo, bounding with great hops across the landscape, and the flightless emu, scurrying along the horizon, were to be seen. He found Cooper's creek, the green bed of one of those Australian rivers that begin nowhere and end nowhere, and pressed on, with renewed hopes of finding a great internal sea. Instead he met the harshest and hottest of desert conditions, red sand-dunes and stony desert where flints lacerated his horse's hooves. The temperature rose to 132°F. in the shade and 157°F. in the sun. But still it was cold at night—and in the clear sky the brilliance of the moon was almost as insufferable as the heat of the sun by day. At last, with food and water running short, he and his party had to give up and turn back. And they only just made it. Sturt returned to Adelaide carried by his companions on a stretcher.

Sturt had, at any rate, penetrated into the interior, geographically almost exactly into the centre. Others followed. A German botanist called Ludwig Leichhardt travelled across the tropical north and then started on a journey from east coast to west. He never returned.

Nobody had yet made the crossing from east to west or north to south. To the bare challenge there was, in addition, a practical inducement. The young Australian colonies were still divided from Britain by a two-months' sea journey. But if a telegraph line could be laid from Adelaide or Melbourne to the northern coast, a link could then be made with the line that already ran through India into south-east Asia and communication with the mother country established.

Adelaide or Melbourne? The state of South Australia or the state of Victoria? Which was to gain the distinction, and the advantage, of first opening up the continent from south to north? By 1860 it had become a race.

One of Sturt's companions had been a small and wiry Scotsman by the name of John McDouall Stuart. This man set off early in 1860 from Adelaide, via Fort Augusta, to cross the continent. The Victorians were not slow in accepting the challenge. Their man was Robert O'Hara Burke; and Burke chose William John Wills as his assistant. The epic of Burke and Wills, of how they reached the northern coast and of what happened to them when they returned to Cooper's creek, is known to every Australian.*

Burke was thirty-nine and Irish; he had been a soldier and was now a police officer, holding down the exacting job of superintendent of a nearby mining area. He was big, handsome and commanding, and though he had no experience in exploring he had a great reputation for dare-devil forcefulness. William John Wills was a complete contrast. He was a keen and efficient young scientist at the Melbourne observatory, twenty-six years old, meticulous and serious-minded. He welcomed with enthusiasm this chance to go on the expedition as astronomer, surveyor and second-in-command.

By August 1860 the excitement in Melbourne was intense. The *Melbourne Punch* published a cartoon showing the dapper McDouall Stuart on a pony and the bearded O'Hara Burke on a towering camel, rushing across the page above the caption, "The Great Australian Exploration Race." On 20 August the expedition

---

*It is told in full, and for all time, by Alan Moorehead in *Cooper's Creek* (Hamish Hamilton 1963). Moorehead followed the course of the expedition in preparation for the writing of this book.

was seen off. There was ceremonial speech-making, and one policeman got knocked over by a camel. By the afternoon the dozen or so principals on their horses, the sepoys specially employed to lead the camels, and the camels specially imported to carry the twenty-one tons of baggage and equipment, all at last left Melbourne.

The first leg of the journey, to Menindie on the Darling river, was through comparatively civilized country and the expedition's only real difficulty was its own cumbersomeness. Burke intended to adopt Sturt's method of forming bases, or depots, and pushing forward from them with smaller parties. But the expedition was obviously over-weighted. At Menindie Burke dismissed, or accepted the resignation of, five men and, without even waiting for his tail-end to catch up, dumped much of his food and equipment and set out again with an advance party of only eight men. He was making for his next base, Cooper's creek. To guide him there

he enlisted a new man, William Wright, an unemployed ranch manager whom he had picked up on the way and liked. Wright was illiterate, but a skilled traveller in the wilderness, a good bushman, as the Australians say.

When they had covered 200 miles Burke, rather surprisingly, sent Wright back. He was to take despatches to Menindie, whence they would go by post to Melbourne; he was to pick up some more of the dumped stores; and then he was to return as soon as possible and catch Burke up at Cooper's creek.

The party covered the remaining 200 miles in good time and soon reached Cooper's creek. Despite heat and thirst, Wills declared that so far it had been a picnic. Well content, they settled down in this pleasant place of blue-gum trees, green grass and meandering waters, to refresh their beasts and to wait for William Wright.

Wright did not turn up.

Burke, thinking perhaps more of his committee's instruction to hurry rather than of their added proviso to be circumspect, decided to push on again with a further reduced party. He left William Brahe as officer-in-charge of the base at Cooper's creek. Brahe, a settler of German extraction, had been promoted from the rank-and-file because of his superior intelligence and education. He was, of course, bitterly disappointed at not being chosen to accompany his chief, but loyally took on this unexpected responsibility. Burke, before leaving, gave him careful instructions, but they were only verbal not written. As Brahe understood them, he was to stay at Cooper's creek awaiting Burke's return for a period of three months or until for lack of food he could not stay any longer. Burke stressed, however, that he himself would have to be back within three months at the most, for his own food would not last him longer than that.

The final party for the race to the northern coast was now ready to depart. It consisted of four men only: Burke and young Wills, and two more men from the rank-and-file, John King and Charley Gray. Gray, an ex-sailor and the oldest of the party, had been recruited by Burke on the way up to Menindie. King, an ex-soldier of twenty-two and the youngest of the party, was in charge of the camels.

At dawn on Sunday, 16 December 1860, nearly four months after they had started and one month after their arrival at Cooper's creek, the little band of four men set out. They had with them six camels and one horse, but the animals were loaded with water and concentrated food and were not for riding. It was 700 miles to the nearest point on the coast of the gulf of Carpentaria, and 700 miles back.

On and on they trudged, first over the hard stony desert that Sturt had traversed, through the wind-blown red dust and an eternal plague of flies, over rugged hills where the camels groaned and sweated in fear. They met the blackfellows, the aborigines, who

William John Wills (1834–61).

though afraid of the camels were inclined to be friendly, indeed sometimes so friendly that their importunities and their gentle art of thieving had to be discouraged by a warning pistol shot. At last, after 500 miles, they approached the tropics where swamp and slime replaced stones and dust, and continual humid heat the cold of nights. Here again the camels were not at all happy and one had to be left behind.

They reached a point about thirty miles from the sea. It was apparent that the camels could go no farther. Leaving King and Gray behind, Burke and Wills loaded themselves and their one horse, Billy, with what rations they could carry and set out to finish the job. The poor horse was almost as much bother as he was worth, having to be pulled and pushed out of mud holes. They met natives who gave them yams and told them the way. Flocks of geese and pelicans, disturbed by their approach, rose into the air. As night fell they reached a channel of water. They tasted it, and it was brackish; they made camp and watched it. It rose—it had a tide. They had reached the sea!

Burke and Wills returned safely to their companions. They had taken the best part of two months out of the three that had been allotted to them, and they had eaten over two-thirds of their rations.

So far, except for having struck the rainy season in the tropics, they had been reasonably lucky. Now luck deserted them.

The rain increased; they had no tents and their clothes were beginning to rot. Some days were so wet that the camels could not move. The four men all began to suffer from head pains and pains in the back and a fearful lassitude. Charley Gray was the worst, and they thought he was exaggerating his ills, "gammoning", to get out of his fair share of duties.

There was one lucky day when they found the camel they had had to leave behind. But the heart had gone out of the beast and he only lasted four days more.

Then there was the day when they killed a huge black snake and, copying the natives, ate some of it—and were ill.

One day it was found that Charley Gray had been stealing the rations. King said later that he was thrashed by Burke, but Wills that he only got some hard slaps on the ear.

By the fortieth day they had completed half of their journey back to base. Already the promised total of three months was past. But at least they had left the enervating tropics.

Gray got no better. Strangely, inhumanly, they still believed he was gammoning; but they let him ride one of the camels. By now they were gradually discarding their equipment, to make the burden lighter for man and beast. Only very occasionally do they seem to have succeeded in shooting any game. At intervals they killed off a camel, eating and "jerking" (cutting into strips and drying) what they could. On the fifty-second day Billy the horse had to go.

On the fifty-ninth day Charley Gray died. He had not been gammoning after all. They dug him a grave, and, so weak were they, it took them all day to do it.

They struggled on, over the stony desert, making at least some progress every day but suffering dreadfully from the bitter cold at night. Burke wished he had not been so generous in giving his spare shirts to some of the blackfellows.

At last, with only two camels left alive, with sixty-six days gone, they had by Wills's reckoning—and he was always wonderfully accurate in his reckoning—just thirty miles to go. They determined, despite their weakness, to make one supreme effort and attempt the last lap in one day.

Buoyed up by the hope of food and welcome they continued on into the night. A moon came up. Burke, in the lead, kept saying, "I think I see them!" When at last he knew unmistakably that he was nearing the base he raised the bushman's long-drawn cooee. "Cooee, Brahe! Coo-ee, Patton!" There was no answer, no movement anywhere in the moonlit bush.

But they found the ashes of recently burntout fires, and saw pieces of discarded equipment lying about. Burke, utterly confused, murmured, "I suppose they have shifted to some other part of the creek." But no one really believed that. Brahe and his party had left.

Could Burke have really expected anything else? Logically, no. But humanly, yes. He had made it perfectly clear that by no manner of means would he come back by sea even if by a great chance the opportunity had offered itself. They had taken longer than three months but,

whatever he had said about time, it had never entered his head that they would be cruelly deserted like this.

As the weeks had gone by, poor William Brahe left in charge at Cooper's creek had been thrown into an agony of indecision. He had expected Wright to arrive with further supplies from Menindie. But Wright did not come. There was no news from anywhere, and still the weeks went by. Brahe felt deserted. Then the symptoms of scurvy began to appear. Finally he realized that one of his party, Patton, was perilously near death. The choice to Brahe seemed to be between saving a life and waiting for men who by now must surely be dead. On 21 April 1861 he made his decision and pulled out for Menindie and Melbourne.

That was the date on the note that Burke and his two companions unearthed when, recovering a little from their dazed disappointment, they observed carved on a tree:

DIG
3 FT N.W.

It was also the date of that very day. They had missed salvation by a few hours.

Brahe, perhaps to put the best face on things, had written in his note that though Patton was ill the rest of them were well and they had horses and camels in good condition. This was not true, and it gave the three exhausted men an entirely wrong impression. They decided that they would never have a chance of catching up with Brahe's party and that the effort was not worth making.

Instead, Burke decided that they should make their way along Cooper's creek and then make a short dash across the desert to Mount Hopeless. Despite its forbidding name, civilization lay close behind that place, and it was only 150 miles away. The food left behind by Brahe—all that he had been able to spare—would, they believed, be just enough for the journey. Regretting bitterly that Brahe had perversely taken with him the little store of fresh clothes, the three men set off along the creek the next day with renewed courage and hope.

For fit men the journey should have been possible. But Burke, Wills and King were already utterly exhausted. The creek was not a simple single river, and they often took a wrong channel and had to turn back. They made very slow progress. First one and then the other of their two remaining camels foundered and had to be shot. For a while a party of blackfellows helped them with food, but then they disappeared.

Burke judged that the time had come for them to make their dash across the desert. For six days they tried to dash. There was nothing before them but an empty horizon. At the end of the sixth day they decided to turn back to Cooper's creek, where at least there was greenness.

Then a curious thing happened. All of them heard the sound of a distant explosion, as of a gun. Probably it was rock splitting off some distant cliff through the action of heat. But these men could only think of one thing: a rescue party was coming up behind them! Wills volunteered to go back and find out.

Wills went all the way back to Brahe's camp.

Curious things had been happening there. Brahe, on his way back to Menindie, met Wright who was at long last coming up to Cooper's creek. There had been some good reason for Wright's failure to return before Burke started on his trek to the coast, but none whatever for this fantastically long delay.

Brahe turned back with Wright, and together they surveyed again the deserted depot at Cooper's creek. Neither of them, not even Wright with his bushman training, noticed that anyone had been there. They did not dig up the cache to see whether the store of food had been taken. They went away again, leaving in turn no sign of their visit.

Twenty-four days later Wills arrived. All was apparently as they had left it. So that was that! Wills wrote a message, in case even yet a rescue party might arrive. It read:

Depot Camp, May 30.
We have been unable to leave the creek. Both camels are dead, and our provisions are done. Mr Burke and King are down the lower part of the

creek. I am about to return to them, when we shall probably come up this way. We are trying to live as best we can, like the blacks, but find it hard work. Our clothes are going to pieces fast. Send provisions and clothes as soon as possible.

Wills managed to reach his comrades again. They tried to live like the blacks but it was more than they could manage. They had learnt how to make a kind of flour, *nardoo*, from a certain seed. But the effort of finding it, and then grinding it, pretty well outweighed the energy gained from the food. Nor were they in a state to gain much strength from any food.

Then the blacks, accused of theft, took offence and left them. They tried to carry on in the way they had been taught. At night they were very cold. In spite of all their sufferings they were still very good friends and there was no recrimination, but it was becoming apparent to all of them that they were likely to die.

Young Wills was now the weakest. As their only hope seemed to be in finding the blackfellows again, Wills urged the other two to leave him. They did so, giving him eight days' supply of *nardoo* and taking two days' supply for themselves. The next day Wills wrote to his father that he thought he had four or five days to live.

When Brahe reached Melbourne with no news of the explorers, a rescue party—indeed more than one rescue party—set out. At Cooper's creek camp they found the note that Wills had left there, and made their way down the creek to find the three men. An excited blackfellow hailed them. One of their horses bolted, scattering the blacks and leaving a solitary scarecrow figure. It tottered, threw up its hands in an attitude of prayer, and fell to the ground.

"Who in the name of wonder are you?"

"I am King, sir."

King said that Burke had lasted only three days, and that when two days later he had gone back to Wills with some food he had found him dead also. Then he had managed to find and make friends with the blackfellows again and they had been very kind to him.

A commission of inquiry at Melbourne exonerated Brahe, but blamed Wright for his delay and the feeble-minded exploration committee for allowing it. Burke was found sometimes to have exerted more zeal than prudence, but admiration was expressed for the gallantry and daring shown by him and his two companions, and sorrow for their untimely death. King was nursed back to some semblance of health and rewarded. He lived eleven more years, and then died of tuberculosis.

And the race? It had been won. To Robert Burke and his companions went the distinction of having been the first to cross the continent from sea to sea. John Stuart's expedition, starting sooner and working further to the west, reached almost as far in distance as Burke's, but had had to stop short some 400 miles from the coast. In the following year Stuart tried again, and reached the coast near the site of the present town of Darwin.

Of course it was not really the race that mattered. Burke and Stuart, equally, helped in the opening-up of the vast interior of Australia, and their lead was rapidly followed by other pioneers. Soon the telegraph cable crossed the continent from north to south.

And yet, material success was perhaps not the most important thing. Burke and Wills, Gray and King, showed determination unto death. They have made a story that will not die.

CHAPTER 10

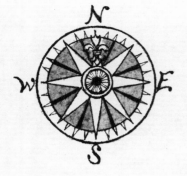

Science and adventure

As THE nineteenth century progressed enormous strides were made in the natural sciences—botany and zoology, geography, geology, anthropology. A new and insistent demand for scientific information therefore arose; and it began to produce a new supply of explorers, men who went out not for gold or gain, not for the glory of their country or for the conversion of the heathen, but simply to acquire scientific knowledge. Yet even if there was a new type of explorer, the pattern of exploration had not really changed. Love of adventure continued to be the powerful incentive.

The geographer Friedrich Heinrich Alexander, Baron von Humboldt—usually known as Alexander Humboldt—was perhaps one of the first explorers of this kind. In 1799 he left the salons and courts of Europe for the vast tropical jungles of the Amazon and Orinoco, where once Orellana and Walter Ralegh had explored. But he was not looking for fabled gold. He was looking for forest flowers and plants; he was looking for evidence that would make the map of that part of the world more accurate.

Humboldt's modern approach did not necessarily make his task much easier. He complained as bitterly as Sir Walter about cramped and uncomfortable conditions: "We had been confined thirty-six days in a narrow boat, so unstable that it would have been overset by any person rising imprudently from his seat. . . . We had suffered severely from the stings of insects." All the more satisfaction, therefore, that he was able to confirm the curious and much disputed story that the two enormous rivers, the Orinoco and the Negro, a tributary of the Amazon, were actually connected by a stream, or natural canal, called the Casiquiari. Humboldt was able to confound the unbelieving armchair geographers for the simple reason that he traversed the whole distance—and we may be sure that he came back with more compelling evidence than insect bites.

Humboldt's interests were extraordinarily wide. He philosophized on the life of the tropical jungle, where man as a species has never had a place, where uninterrupted organic power is manifested in lush vegetation and where the lords of creation are the boa constrictor and the crocodile, the monkey and the jaguar. He collected 60,000 botanical specimens, of which a large proportion were new to the western world. He studied the weather and its causes—then a new field of enquiry. He climbed one of the highest peaks in the Andes. He was the first to point out that volcanoes tended to occur in recognizable lines on the map. He was interested in the fertilizing

properties of guano (the excrement of Peruvian sea birds), and in many other immensely practical matters.

Then he came back to Europe, to write long but readable books and to establish himself as the friend and protector of younger scientists. The tsar of Russia asked him to undertake an exploration in the eastern parts of his empire. At the age of sixty, he duly obliged. He crossed the Urals and then penetrated far beyond into China and the Altai mountains. For himself he accumulated data for his projected isothermic map of the world—and for the tsar he found diamonds.

And for the western world he brought back more information about the secret places and frozen heights of Asia, such as Marco Polo had seen so long ago. Two decades later, in the 1840s, the Abbé Huc, another dedicated French missionary-explorer, was doing the same thing in a terrible and fantastic journey over the mountains to Lhasa.

Charles Montagu Doughty was a geologist. He was one of the many nineteenth-century Europeans who were attracted by Arabia. It became almost an obsession with certain men and women of that time to get away from civilization and share the hard, bitter, brilliant, down-to-sand existence of the bedouin Arab in the emptiness of the desert.

Baron von Humboldt (1769–1859)—one of the first of the scientific explorers.

In the course of his travels in Arabia in the 1870s Doughty gained much information about the geological structure of the country and about its watershed. But his greatest contribution to European knowledge was in the field of anthropology, the science of man's habits, beliefs and customs. In his book *Travels in Arabia Deserta*, which was published in 1888, he revealed the Moslem mind and the bedouin world.

It was an enormous and strangely written work. At first people found it disconcerting, and it really only made an impact when twenty years later it was abridged for the author by a fellow writer, Edward Garnett. Charles Doughty made his mark on the world by his pen, but the material for his writings was not acquired without difficulty. The following excerpt from *Arabia Deserta* describes one of the many perilous moments of his travels. Doughty was being threatened by Salem, an Arabian sherif, or nobleman, who was almost demented in his ferocious hatred of all Christians. His Negro guide Maabub was not there to help him.

The mad sherif had the knife again in his hand! and his old gall rising, "Show me all that thou hast," cries he, "and leave nothing; or now will I kill thee."—Where was Maabub? whom I had not seen since yester-evening: in him was the faintness and ineptitude of Arab friends.—"Remember the bread and salt which we have eaten together, Salem!"—"Show it all to me, or by Allah I will slay thee with this knife." More bystanders gathered from the shadowy places: some of them cried out, "Let us hack him in morsels, the cursed one! what hinders?—fellows, let us hack him in morsels!"—"Have patience a moment, and send these away." Salem, lifting his knife, cried, "Except thou show me all at the instant, I will slay thee!" But rising and a little retiring from them I

T.E.—H

said *"Let none think to take away my pistol!"*—
which I drew from my bosom.

What should I do now? the world was before me;
I thought, Shall I fire, if the miscreants come upon
me; and no shot amiss? I might in the first horror
reload—my thelul [riding camel] *was at hand: and*
if I could break away from more than a score of
persons, what then? . . .

Doughty did not fire, and to this he probably
owed his life, though it undoubtedly pro-
longed his agonizing predicament. The pistol
was handed over and shot off into the air. Only
an assumed air of tranquillity, and a long sermon
to the sherif on how the law would surely
catch up with him if he were to commit
murder, saved Doughty. A highly distinctive
author was saved by his own courage from a
premature grave, and from him Europeans
learned to understand a little better the strange
world in the desert heart of Arabia.

From Mary Kingsley's lively anthropological
studies Europeans learned to understand a little
better the strange world in the jungle heart of
western Africa.

Mary Kingsley was surely the most amazing
and the most amusing of all the explorers. To
the modern world this woman who wandered
alone about Africa in long Victorian skirts and
with her umbrella is a joke. She, too, considered her own experiences as a huge joke.
Yet she was passionately serious: and, what is
more, she convinced important people that she
was serious, and eventually she began to
exercise almost as great an influence on English
colonial policy in Africa as Livingstone had
done.

Mary had a selfish father who pleased himself by being nearly always away from home, a
mother who was increasingly dependent on her
as an invalid, and a brother on whom the

family's spare income was totally spent. She
once wrote that the only paid-for education *she*
ever received was lessons in German—and that
was her own idea.

But Mary was no more an ordinary child
than she was to be an ordinary person. She was
a Kingsley. Her family had a long tradition of
adventurousness; and, moreover, it had just
produced three exciting men whom she
greatly admired. Charles Kingsley, her uncle,
was the famous novelist, naturalist, propa-
gandist and exponent of "muscular Christianity". Henry, another uncle who used to come
and stay with them, was a writer, and had been
a gold prospector, a cowboy, a miner and a
mounted policeman. And George Kingsley,
her father, was an extraordinary character. He
could never settle down, and never tried to.
He was a doctor but, like Mungo Park, found
domestic doctoring too dull for him. He therefore became private physician to rich noblemen
whose idea of a good life was to travel in
strange parts or go big-game hunting. He was
horribly unfair to his family, driving his wife
into ill health from responsibility and worry
and condemning his daughter to a narrow life
as nurse and housekeeper. His letters home,
however, were marvellous, and when he did
himself come home then *everything* was marvellous, at least so thought the growing girl,

who worshipped him as he did not deserve to be worshipped.

And then the books that Mary's father possessed! She had to be careful not to be reading them when he wanted them, but otherwise they were all hers. She read difficult books on physics and medicine, and ancient and modern books on travel. She became interested in chemistry, and tried to teach herself mathematics. One of her favourite books, *The Pursuit of Knowledge Under Difficulties*, fitted her own problem exactly.

Mary grew up into womanhood. Her mother became even more of an exacting invalid, and her father, at home a little more often, got her to help him in translating the works of certain German anthropologists in whom he was interested. She was interested too. But she was very lonely.

Then in 1892 her parents died, within a few weeks of each other; her brother went away for reasons of health; and she found herself, at the age of thirty, with no responsibilities and an adequate income of £500 a year. Her real life could start.

A year later, Mary Kingsley embarked at Liverpool for the west coast of Africa.

Why there? She had, she explained, some anthropological work to finish for her father, and so she went to where native Africans were "at their wildest and worst". "It was," she explained, "no desire to get killed and eaten that made me go and associate with the tribes with the worst reputation for cannibalism and human sacrifice, but just because such tribes were the best for me to study for what they meant by doing such things." They also, no doubt, afforded the best contrast to Victorian domesticity and supplied the risk, hardship, excitement and danger that she subconsciously wanted. The British Museum authorities, somewhat patronizingly, commissioned her to bring back specimens of marine and insect life—and they were amazed at the quality of her efforts.

Mary Kingsley made two journeys in western Africa, in the region of the Ogowe river, which flows between the Niger of Mungo Park and the Congo of Livingstone and Stanley (it was in this area that Dr Schweitzer later established his famous hospital). No white man, and certainly no white women, had ever explored here before.

In her accounts of her travels Mary was always making fun of herself and light of her difficulties. She explained, for instance, that Victorian skirts were very useful as a cushion when you fell into a spiked pit meant for big game. But it would be a very insensitive reader who did not realize that she was continually meeting the most appalling difficulties and dangers.

The people she elected to consort with and study were the Fan tribe, a cannibal tribe of notorious ferocity. She survived by means of sweet reasonableness coupled with transparent goodwill and honesty. With the medical knowledge she had picked up, and it was probably considerable, she helped people wherever she could. She posed as a trader, indeed she

acted as a trader; and she earned respect by driving hard bargains but never cheating.

On one occasion she met a leopard, and told it to "go home, you fool!" so severely, but reasonably, that it went. On another occasion, when she was exploring in mangrove swamps, a crocodile got its forelegs over the edge of her canoe. "I had to retire to the bows to keep the balance right (it is no use saying because I was frightened, for this miserably understates the case), and fetch him a clip on the snout with a paddle." In the mangrove swamps she had to keep a motherly eye—they called her "Ma"—on her somewhat careless crew. "On one examination I found the leg of one of my most precious men ostentatiously sticking out over the side of the canoe. I woke him with a paddle, and said a few words regarding the inadvisability of wearing his leg like this in our situation; and he agreed with me, saying he had lost a valued uncle who had been taken out of a canoe in this same swamp by a crocodile. His uncle's ghost had become, he said, a sort of devil which had been a trial to the family ever since; and he thought it must have pulled his leg out in the way I complained of, in order to get him to join him by means of another crocodile. I thanked him for the information and said it quite explained the affair. . . . "

Her first introduction to the fierce and cannibal Fans was an abrupt one. She fell through the roof of a hut that was concealed in a hollow. "What the unfortunate inhabitants were doing, I don't know, but I am pretty sure they were not expecting me to drop in, and a scene of great confusion occurred. My knowledge of Fan dialect then consisted of 'Kor Kor', and so I said that in as fascinating a tone as I could, and explained the rest with three pocket handkerchiefs, a head of tobacco and a knife, which providentially I had stowed away in what my nautical friends would call my after-hold—my pockets." This was another recommendation for Victorian skirts, at any rate as worn by Mary Kingsley. "Remember," she observed, "that whenever you see a man, black or white, filled with a nameless longing, it is tobacco he requires." Alternatively, it may be something wrong with his pipe, in which case you offer him a straightened-out hairpin.

But Mary was not always joking. She did not, she said, really recommend African forest life to anyone. "Unless you are interested in it and fall under its charm, it is the most awful life-in-death imaginable. It is like being shut up in a library whose books you cannot read, all the while tormented, terrified, and bored."

Mostly, nevertheless, she undoubtedly enjoyed herself. One part of her progress up the Ogowe river she described as luxurious, charming and pleasant. "The men are standing up, swinging in rhythmic motion their long, rich, red-wood paddles in perfect time to their elaborate, melancholy minor-key boat song." As enjoyable, in another way, was the excitement when they met the rapids and she had to leap out of the boat and cling to a rock face. As for the Fans, this was no sentimental attachment—she always carried a revolver and a knife about with her. "We each recognized that we belonged to the same section of the human race with whom it is better to drink than to fight. We knew we would each have killed the other if sufficient inducement were offered, and so we took a certain amount of care that the inducement should not arise."

And so this amazing tough-tender woman came home, and wrote her book and articles for the papers, and lectured up and down the country, and talked to people who mattered, including the colonial secretary. She had penetrated a little way into the West African mind—a very difficult task and one that no explorer before her, except perhaps Livingstone, had even tried to accomplish—and she did her best to pass on her knowledge.

At the outbreak of the Boer war Mary gave up her plan of returning to West Africa, and unwillingly but dutifully responded to the call for nurses. In 1900 she died of enteric fever in her Cape Town hospital: she was thirty-eight years old.

The last great exploration into completely unknown territory—polar exploration apart—was probably that undertaken by Colonel

P. H. Fawcett in the Mato Grosso area of South America at the beginning of this century.

Fawcett was the born explorer. Throughout his career in the regular army he kept his body fit and his mind trained in order that one day he might explore. His first chance came in 1906, when he was thirty-nine. The Royal Geographical Society nominated him for service with the Bolivian government, to assist them in the defining of their boundaries vis-à-vis their neighbours, Brazil and Peru, in the huge unknown forest area south of the Amazon, the Mato Grosso.

Fawcett spent many years on the job, occasionally returning to the civilized towns on the coast before making yet another bold incision into the resistant body of the continent. His work, which probably prevented many minor wars between these jealous South American states, was a constant struggle against the enmity of the Indian natives and the inhospitality and dangers of the jungle.

In 1908, after a long and difficult journey, Fawcett penetrated to the source of the Rio Verde (the green river) which now forms part of the boundary between Bolivia and Brazil. Above him towered the Ricardo Franco hills, flat-topped, mysterious and unreachable—Conan Doyle was to make them the setting of his story, *The Lost World*. Behind him lay the route by which he had come, through hostile country where he and his party had nearly died of starvation. He decided to push on. Among steep canyons, dogged always by ill luck, the little expedition soon found itself at the end of its resources.

On October 13th, feeling that we had come to our last gasp, I did what I had never known to fail when the need was sufficiently pronounced, and that is to pray audibly for food. Not kneeling, but turning

Colonel P. H. Fawcett—the last of the romantics.

east and west, I called for assistance—forcing myself to know that assistance would be forthcoming. In this way did I pray, and within fifteen minutes a deer showed itself in a clearing three hundred yards away.

The others saw it at the same time, and a breathless silence fell as I unslung my rifle. It was almost hopeless range for a violently kicking Winchester carbine; and at the end of one's tether from hunger or thirst the sight is not reliable, nor is it easy to hold the rifle steady.

*"For God's sake don't miss, Fawcett!" The hoarse whisper came from close behind me. Miss! As I sighted along the shaking barrel I knew the bullet would find its mark. The power that answered my prayer would see that it did. Never have I made a cleaner kill—the animal dropped with severed spine where it stood.**

from Operation Fawcett by P. H. Fawcett, edited by Brian Fawcett (Hutchinson 1953).

It was the turning point of the expedition, the prelude to a happy ending. Fawcett was always sanguine, always romantic, and he always believed in his luck—which in the end deserted him.

In the course of these boundary-defining expeditions Colonel Fawcett became, slowly but steadily, more and more obsessed by one particular idea. Like Orellana and Ralegh, he believed in an El Dorado. His El Dorado was, like theirs, a lost city of the ancient American civilizations, but it was historical interest and not gold that inspired him to search for it.

At long last, in 1924, he collected the necessary financial backing and set off for his lost city. He was fifty-five. He took with him his elder son and his son's friend, both in their early twenties. Fawcett did not believe in

*The mysterious Ricardo Franco hills—
a challenge to explorers.*

elaborate and large expeditions; he believed in
his own skill as a pathfinder, in his own power
of making friends with the natives, and in his
own luck.

His younger son, Brian, tells the story of the
search for the lost city at the end of *Operation
Fawcett*. To put it with brutal shortness, the
expedition went into the Amazonian jungle
and never came out. It was never heard of
again.

Several attempts were made to find the
missing explorers, and strange stories were
brought back. It was said that a queer, silent,
tattered, white-haired man was living somewhere in the interior as the prisoner of a native
tribe. A pale-skinned, blue-eyed baby was

found and it was thought to be the child of Fawcett's eldest son. But the baby turned out to be a native albino; and the old man was never found. The hope of discovering exactly what did happen to Fawcett and his companions lingers on; but it is generally assumed that they all perished at the hands of hostile natives.

With the tragic but romantic and mysterious end of the Fawcett expedition we come to the end of a whole era of exploration. Fawcett might be called the last of the old school, the last of the romantics—and something of an anachronism at that. And it is a strange but perhaps significant coincidence that one of the most modern of explorations in the 1960s should be taking place in the same area that was the scene of Fawcett's brave, risky, scientifically improvident efforts. The Brazilian government has invited scientists from many countries to study the flora and fauna of the Mato Grosso before the building of a new road alters its character for ever. The British Royal Geographical Society has set up a well-equipped base camp 160 miles beyond Xavantina in the state of Mato Grosso, and from there continually changing teams of experts do stints of intensive field-work in the neighbourhood.

Exploration can, in fact, now be described as the scientific study of environment. It is not necessarily less heroic, though it is different.

It is still adventure.

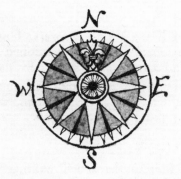

The books in this list should be obtainable from your county or municipal library. If they are not immediately available on the library shelves or in the stock-room the librarian will arrange to get them for you from another library—a remarkable service for which we ought to be truly grateful.

Details of publisher and date of publication are not given except to indicate that a book can be bought cheaply in a paperback edition or that it is not modern—and this you should mention when you make enquiries at the library. Asterisks are used to denote books that are generally classified as children's books.

GENERAL

For those who wish to read the first-hand accounts—and they could not do better—*The*

Explorers, an Anthology by G. R. Crone will act as introduction and guide. *A Book of Discovery*★ (well illustrated) by M. R. Synge (1912), *The World and its Discovery* by H. B. Wetherill (1914) and the more recent *Exploring the World* by Stella Davies cover both exploration and discovery.

CHAPTER 1

The first three chapters of *The Great Invasion* by Leonard Cottrell (Pan Books Ltd 1961) give an interesting account of Caesar's visits to Britain.

CHAPTER 2

Marco Polo's travels are published in the Everyman series and in the Penguin Classics. There is also *The Story of Marco Polo*★ by

O. Price and *They Went with Marco Polo*★ by Louise Kant. H. G. Wells, in his *Short History of the World* (published as a Penguin) and in his longer *Outline of History* explains the significance of the rise of the Mongols and the supremacy of eastern civilization at that time.

CHAPTER 3

Prescott's *Conquest of Mexico* is in the Everyman series, and Bernal Diaz's narrative is in Penguin Classics. Maurice Collis explains the actions of Montezuma very clearly in his *Cortes and Montezuma*. There is also *Cortes, Conqueror of Mexico*★ by Ronald Syme, and Rider Haggard's exciting tale, *Montezuma's Daughter*.

CHAPTER 4

Prescott's *Conquest of Peru* is also in the Everyman series. *The Conquistadors* by Jean Descola gives a comprehensive account of all these Spanish adventurers. *The River of No Return*★ by Ronald Syme tells of the exploration of the Amazon. There is a sympathetic life of Ralegh by Aubrey de Selincourt; and Rosemary Sutcliff has written a romantic novel, *Lady in Waiting*, about Ralegh and his wife.

CHAPTER 5

On early Virginia I recommend *Red Man's Country*★ by P. Rush and *The Story of Pocahontas*★ by S. Graham. *The Explorers of North America* by J. B. Brebuer covers the whole field. Louise Kant has written *They Went with Champlain*★ and Ronald Syme, *La Salle of the Mississippi*.

CHAPTER 6

Mackenzie appears in *Great Explorers*★ by N. Wymer, and Thompson is the hero of *The Map Maker*★ by Kerry Wood. Stewart's book, *The Californian Trail*, which is mentioned in this chapter, and *Death on the Prairie* by Paul Wellman make good reading. Fenimore Cooper's story, *The Last of the Mohicans*, will tell you a good deal about Red Indians.

CHAPTERS 7 and 8

As an introduction to the actual writings of the African explorers there is, besides G. R. Crone's book mentioned in the general section at the beginning of this list, another anthology called *African Discovery* by Margery Perham and J. Simmons. Mungo Park's *Travels* is in the Everyman series, and Ronald Syme has written *I, Mungo Park*. Robin Maugham tells of his own adventures, as well as those of his predecessors, on a journey to Timbuctoo in *The Slaves of Timbuctoo*. Alan Moorehead has written two fine books on the exploration of the Nile, *The White Nile* and *The Blue Nile*. Rider Haggard's novels about Alan Quartermaine give a romanticized picture of the life of an African explorer. There is also *With Stanley in Africa*★ by O. Hall Guest.

CHAPTER 9

The great book here is *Cooper's Creek* by Alan Moorehead. *Australian Discovery* by E. Scott covers the whole field.

CHAPTER 10

I suggest that you read *Alexander Humboldt*★ by M. Z. Thomas and *Mary Kingsley*★ by C. Clair. Doughty's life has been written by D. G. Hogarth. As well as *Exploration Fawcett*, edited by Brian Fawcett, there is a chapter on Fawcett that you should read in *Six Great Travellers*★ by J. L. Cook.

Index

A number in italic denotes that a principal reference begins on that page.